AF589105

LOG CABIN QUILT BLOCKS

100 colour and pattern variations

LOG CABIN QUILT BLOCKS

100 colour and pattern variations

Catherine-Marie Longtin

Photography by Tom Leighton

BATSFORD

First published in the United Kingdom
in 2026 by
Batsford
43 Great Ormond Street
London
WC1N 3HZ

An imprint of B. T. Batsford Holdings Limited

Photography by Tom Leighton (with the exception of pages 6 and 207)

ISBN 978 1 84994 989 7

A CIP catalogue record for this book is available from the British Library.

10 9 8 7 6 5 4 3 2 1

Reproduction by Rival Colour Ltd, UK
Printed by Toppan Leefung Printing International Ltd, China

This book can be ordered direct from the publisher at www.batsfordbooks.com, or try your local bookshop

Distributed throughout the UK and Europe by Abrams & Chronicle Books, 1st Floor, 22–24 Ely Place, London EC1N 6TE and 57 rue Gaston Tessier, 75166 Paris, France

www.abramsandchronicle.co.uk
info@abramsandchronicle.co.uk

CONTENTS

Catherine-Marie Longtin. Block Variations. 'Quilts: A Material Culture' exhibition at B.T. Batsford Gallery. London, May 2023. Photo by Tim Crocker.

INTRODUCTION

The log cabin is one of the oldest patchwork blocks, and one of the first piecing techniques taught in quilting classes. It's a simple way to build a block: you take a square centre, then make it bigger by adding fabric strips on all sides until you reach the desired size. But, although the basic idea is simple, it lends itself to infinite variations. A few years ago, I explored some of these variations for an exhibition called 'Quilts: A Material Culture' at the B.T. Batsford Gallery in East London. While I didn't specifically set out with this in mind, 14 out of the 16 square artworks ended up being log cabin blocks. I was excited to be able to experiment freely: it felt liberating to work on a small scale and create individual blocks that didn't have to match or be part of a quilt. It was also a chance to create colour studies, and I enjoyed thinking not only about each colour within one block but also about how the colours of all the blocks would interact once on the wall. I was hooked, and looked for a project that would allow me to explore the possibilities of the log cabin in a systematic way. And that is how this book came about.

I started by mapping all the variations that came to my mind on squared paper. Then I organized these blocks into groups, weeding out ones that looked a bit too similar to others or didn't bring much to the conversation. Once I had 100 blocks, I numbered them from 1 to 100 and set out to make them in this order, following a colour story that unfolded in my head, in the studio and now on these pages.

The first 11 blocks show the possibilities within the basic pattern: start with a one inch centre and add one inch strips, but vary the arrangement of colours. Then more complex variations are introduced, by playing with different elements and parameters: width of strips, size and complexity of the centres, cornerstones, double lines, curves, etc. Some variations are very traditional, others less so. Some blocks did not turn out as I expected them to, others only revealed themselves once several rounds of strips were added. I could have made a thousand block variations; 100 felt like a good place to start.

Blocks

BLOCK 1 (FRONT)

BLOCK 1 (BACK)

BLOCK 14 (BACK)

BLOCK 28

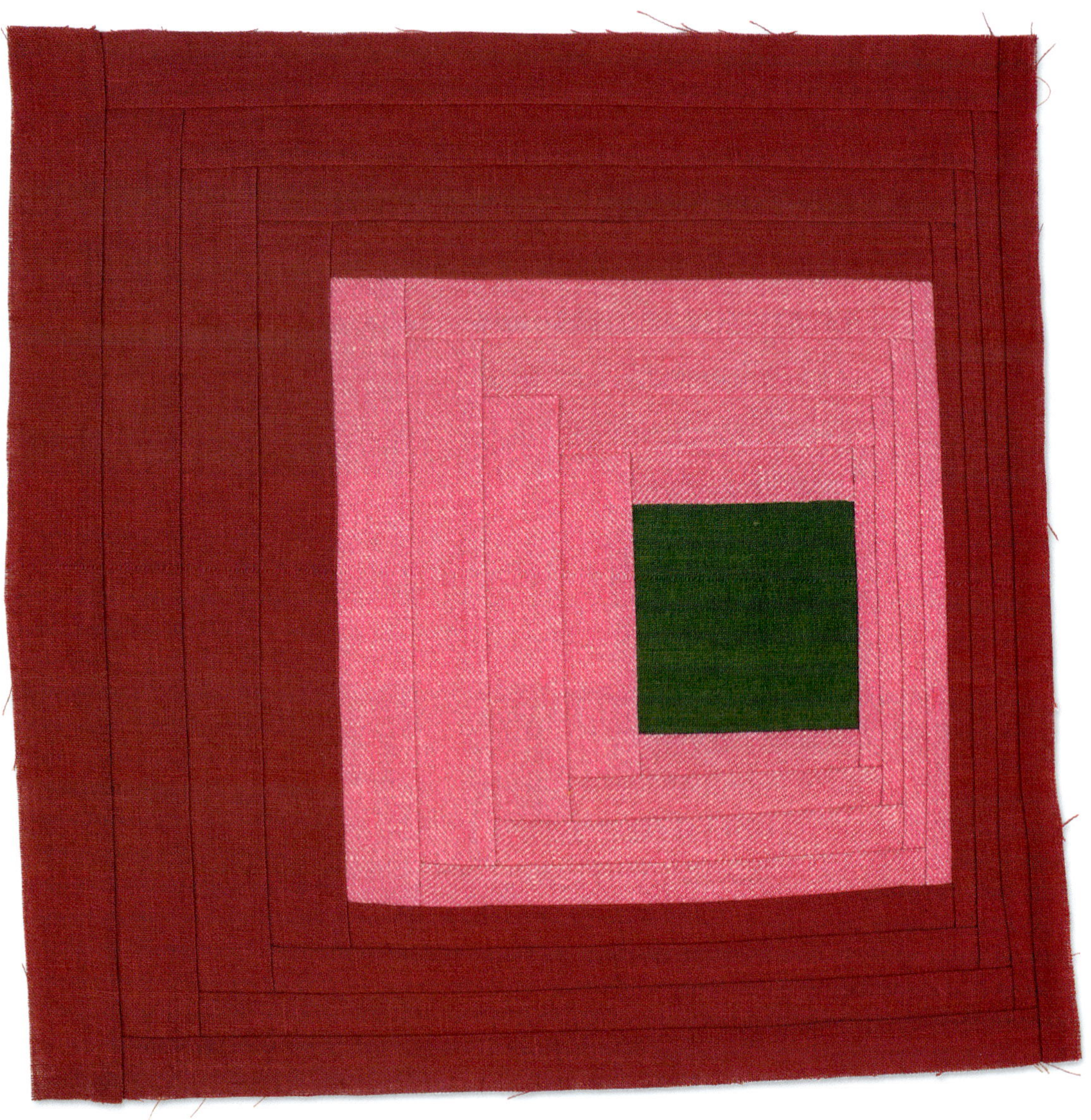

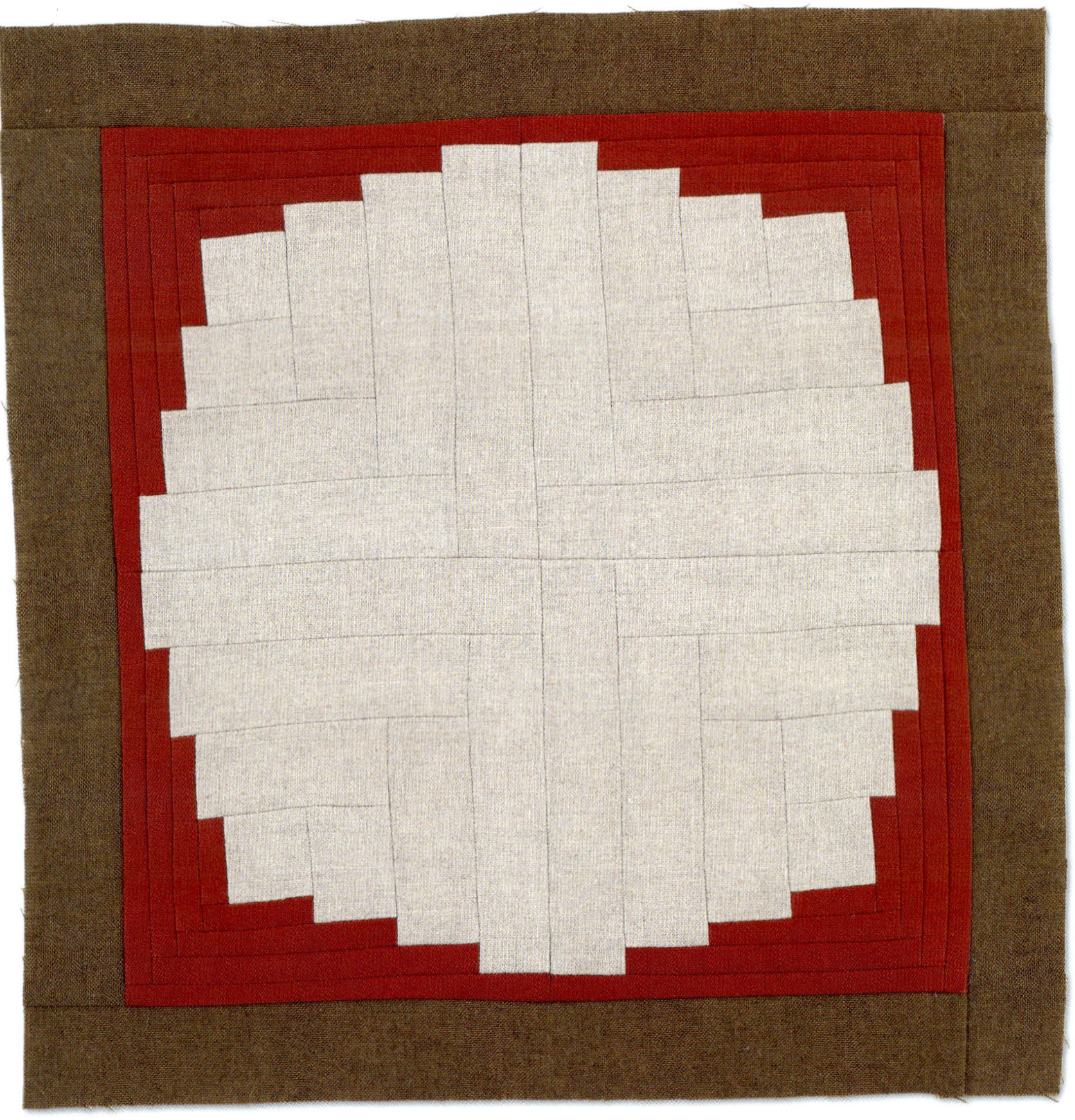

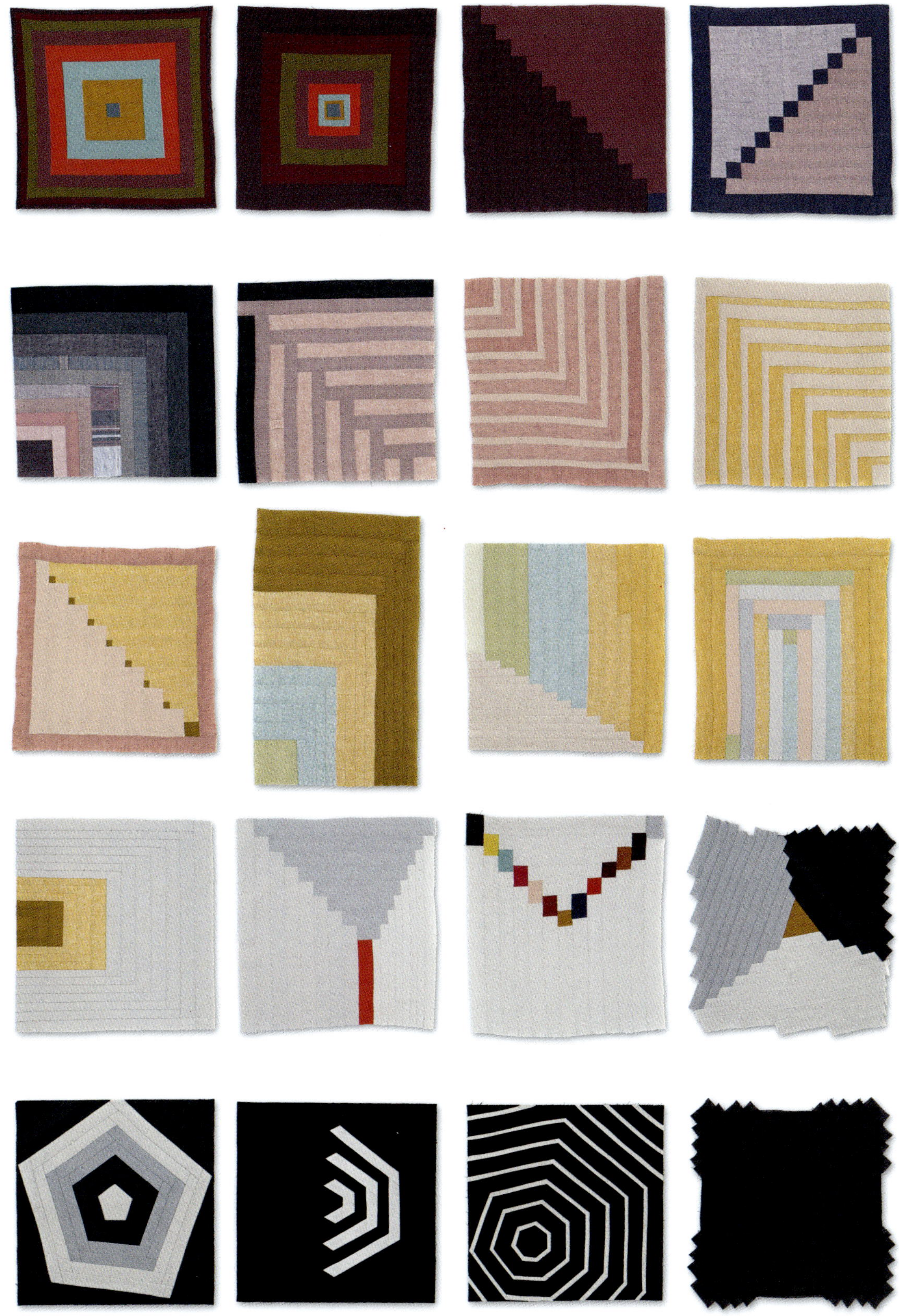

CLOTH
JOSEF ALBERS
PFAFF

Method

BEFORE YOU START

If you have never done patchwork before, don't be intimidated by the patterns and complexities in some of the blocks in this book, or by preconceived ideas of what a quilt should look like. I tell participants in my workshops that if they are capable of sewing two pieces of fabric together then they are capable of doing patchwork. The basic log cabin is one of the easiest quilt blocks to make, and you will get great results very quickly. Have a read through the Basic Skills section on page 134, follow the instructions on how to make a block with the Basic Method on page 143 and you will soon have a complete first block. Everything else is optional.

If it doesn't quite work the first time, you'll have learnt something – just try again. There's sheer pleasure in seeing a log cabin block grow, one round after the other, and it's very much worth persevering. It's also worth remembering that a wonky block is not a failed block. Attitudes to wonkiness vary widely within the quilting community, ranging from quilters for whom accuracy is everything and who will only accept millimetre precision in their work, to those who will actively seek out wobbly lines and irregular shapes. I stand somewhere in the middle: while I don't set out to sew wonky blocks, I don't always go out of my way to achieve precision. There's humanity and beauty in imperfection, which I highly value in other quilters' work and have learnt to embrace in my own. Sometimes wonky *is* perfection.

And, lastly, give yourself permission to explore and experiment. Quilters have invented patterns and played with traditions for centuries – now it's your turn.

NOTIONS AND MATERIALS

NOTIONS

You will need the following to make the blocks in this book:

- Cutting mat with plexiglass ruler (if you haven't bought one already, look for a mat and ruler with inches, as imperial measurements are widely used in quilting)
- Rotary cutter with spare blades
- Sewing machine
- Scissors
- Seam ripper
- Iron and ironing board
- Pins
- Small ruler
- Seam roller (optional)
- Graph paper, pencil and eraser to design your own blocks

FABRIC

I used linen, cotton and cotton-linen blends for all the blocks in this book. Some of the fabrics I bought new, others are vintage fabrics that were given to me, remnants from clothes making or old pieces of clothing that I have cut up. I prefer on the whole to work with natural fibres, and I am particularly fond of fabrics that have a bit of texture, like linen, or a two-tone effect, like chambrays and shot cottons (where the weave and the weft are different coloured threads).

Don't feel constrained to use a single type of fabric or to stick to quilting cottons when doing patchwork. Traditionally, quilting was a way to use up bits of fabric that were too small for clothes making or to repurpose old or damaged clothes and house linens. Look around at what you already have, be open minded about trying different types of fabrics and don't worry too much about mixing fibres.

This being said, there are a few things that are worth considering before you start. Firstly, think about what you intend to do with your block. If you wish to use it in a quilt, then it's worth using materials that will wash well and withstand the wear and tear of everyday use. If you are going to use your block in a decorative quilt hanging or a framed artwork then your choice of materials will matter less. In the same vein, consider the weight of the fabrics you use, and whether it's appropriate for your project to mix different weights. A lightweight cotton lawn, for instance, will thin and tear faster than a quilting cotton or a linen, which will shorten the lifespan of a quilt made with both.

If you don't already have a stash of fabrics, it helps to have access to a good fabric store, but short of that there are lots of online stores that offer a wide variety of materials. Some of them have a fabric remnant section, where you will be able to find smaller cuts at discounted prices. Charity shops are also an excellent place to look for fabrics: you can purchase second hand clothes cheaply and use the fabric for quilting. Also look for table cloths, bed linens and tea towels.

Preparing your fabric for sewing

Unless you only intend to make wall hangings and framed artworks, it is generally a good idea to prewash all your fabrics to avoid shrinking and colours bleeding once they are sewn together and quilted. The common advice is to follow the manufacturer's instructions and prewash your fabric in the same way you intend to wash the clothes/quilts, making sure you keep light and dark colours separate. I machine wash cottons in warm water (40 degrees Celsius; or 'warm') and linens in cold-warm water (30 degrees Celsius, or 'cold-warm' on some machines). I use the lowest spinning speed and hang the fabrics to dry, as high speed spinning and the tumble dryer can leave permanent marks on the surface, especially on linens. Fabrics that are dry-clean only can be used as is.

THREAD

There are a variety of machine sewing threads available, and while most of them will do the job, it's worth looking for a good quality thread that won't break, stretch or produce a lot of lint. I use both cotton thread and polyester thread in my studio, and buy from trusted brands. Beware of cheap polyester thread as it can melt under a hot iron.

For colour, I will choose a thread that matches most of the fabrics in the block. If there are lots of colours together then I will settle for off-white for light coloured fabrics, light to medium grey for medium coloured fabric and medium to dark grey for dark coloured fabrics. Light grey is a good default when mixing light and dark fabrics together.

ON CHOOSING COLOURS

I have been collecting fabrics for over ten years, and have developed a healthy stash of solids which I used for this book. I have always loved to play with colours, from sorting out Skittles and Smarties when I was small to organizing my coloured pencil box and mixing paints in art classes. I love how colours translate into fabrics – I'm constantly learning about what works for me and what doesn't, and I try to challenge myself to learn how to use certain colours that are less obvious to me.

If you are not feeling confident about colours, it's worth spending a bit of time reflecting on what you like and why some colour combinations make your heart sing and others do not. Combining colours is like speaking a language, and there are many colour languages out there. Ultimately you will develop your own, but, in the meantime, start by studying how other people articulate theirs.

A good place to start is observing your own surroundings, starting with your own home. The look of an attractive product is the result of a team of people making conscious decisions about which colour is going to be used, which combination, which shade, in which proportion and it's worth thinking about why some of them catch your eye in a way that others do not. Then look for colour combinations in fashion, interior design, architecture, artworks, prints, nature, etc. Study your favourite artists, look for colours when you wander around a garden, notice the colours of the costumes in your favourite period drama or Wes Anderson film. If you have a thing for birds or, say, mid-century book covers, then that can be your starting point. Printed fabrics are excellent too. I find that most prints from Liberty of London are a colour masterclass: every shade, from the background to the tiniest accent, is carefully considered. If there's a colour combination you particularly like, take note, and try to emulate this palette in your patchwork.

Some social media platforms are very useful for collecting colours: Pinterest will allow you to pin images and organize them in boards, Instagram will let you save posts you like into folders. They are where I go when I need inspiration and ideas about how to use a particular shade. Colour theory and the colour wheel are also useful tools. I find that my favourite colour combinations are often based on adjacent colours (e.g. orange + orange-red; yellow + yellow-green) and what is called split complementary: when two adjacent or near adjacent colours are matched with a third complementary colour (e.g. two shades of blue + orange). While principles of colour theory can explain why some colour combinations work and others do not, it shouldn't override your own likes and dislikes, and an intuitive approach to colour is as valid as anything. If you love it, then that's all that matters.

Unless you are skilled at dyeing fabrics, translating your favourite colour combinations into patchwork will be constrained by the availability of materials, and loving one particular colour combination won't necessarily mean that it's going to be easy to replicate in a block. Quilting cotton solids come in a wide variety of colours, and using fabrics from different producers means that you can find more subtle colour combinations. While one brand might not carry every possible shade of yellow, mixing yellows from three or four manufacturers will add subtle colour variations to your stash. Linen is more difficult to source, and usually shops won't hold as many colours as they would of quilting cotton. Again it's worth shopping around as different shops will have different shades.

All this being said, you do not need an extensive stash to make the blocks in this book. Over half of them use three colours or fewer, and all of them can be made using a limited palette. Some of my favourite quilters only work with four or five colours, and a quick survey of antique quilts will show you that a lot can be done with few colours. My advice is to try things out, play around and avoid overthinking it.

ARCHITECTURE OF THE LOG CABIN

While all blocks in this book are mapped out in the Block Directory on pages 174–204, it is helpful to learn how to 'read' a block, i.e. understand its structure in order to replicate it. This way you can look at any log cabin quilt and figure out how it has been pieced.

SOME VOCABULARY

Centre: The starting point, and the piece around which all the logs will be sewn.

Logs: The patchwork pieces which are sewn around the centre.

Rounds: The number of times you go around the centre, i.e. the number of logs in any of the four directions. In quarter and three-quarter log cabin blocks, a round will only cover two and three sides respectively.

Strips: The long pieces of fabric that are cut to be used as logs in a block. The width of the strip will include the seam allowance. For example, you will need a 1½" (3.8cm) strip of fabric to achieve a 1" (2.5cm) log if you are using a ¼" (0.6cm) seam allowance.

Cornerstones: Squares of contrasting fabric that are used to add a bit of interest to a quilt, added to the end of logs to create a pattern within the block and/or across multiple blocks.

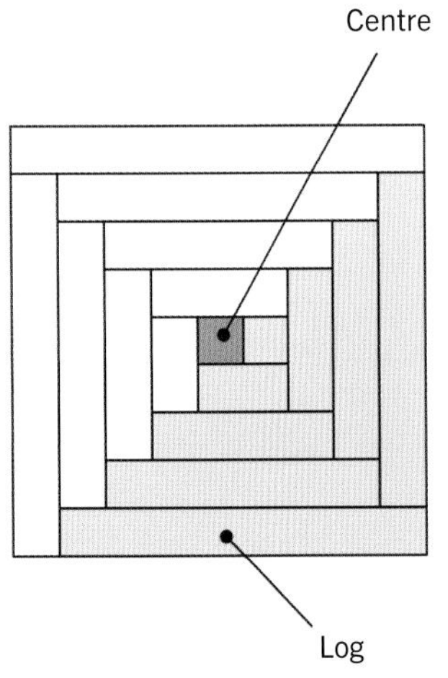

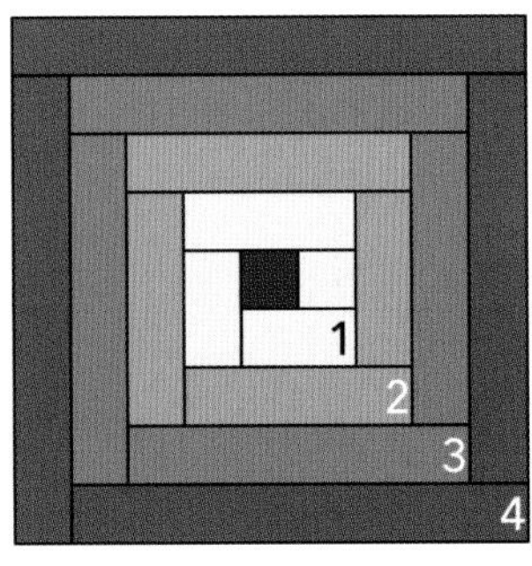

Rounds

PIECING DIRECTION AND TYPES OF BLOCKS

Variations are infinite, but are all founded on the basic principle of a central piece surrounded or partly surrounded by strips of fabric. The order of piecing matters, as well as the distribution of colours, especially when making multiple blocks that are going to be arranged together to create a specific design.

Clockwise and anticlockwise: Strips can be sewn around the centre clockwise or anticlockwise. If you are making a single block this doesn't matter much, but it becomes relevant when you sew multiple blocks that will be arranged together in a particular way. For instance, in some of the circle log cabins (Blocks 86 and 90), two blocks must be pieced clockwise around the centre, and two pieced anticlockwise.

Courthouse steps: Another traditional way to piece a log cabin is the courthouse steps variation, which involves piecing opposite sides of the central square in immediate succession rather than going around the centre. You add logs to the left and right of the centre, then to the top and bottom.

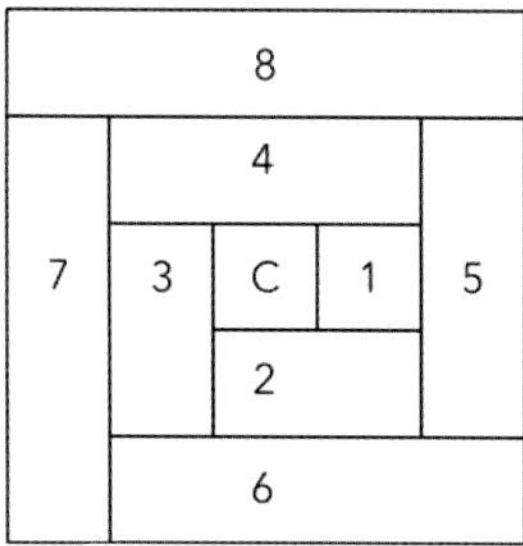

Clockwise

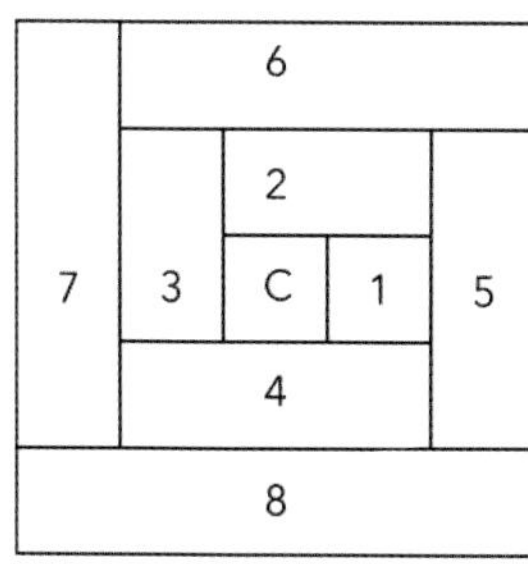

Anticlockwise

C = centre of the block

Courthouse steps

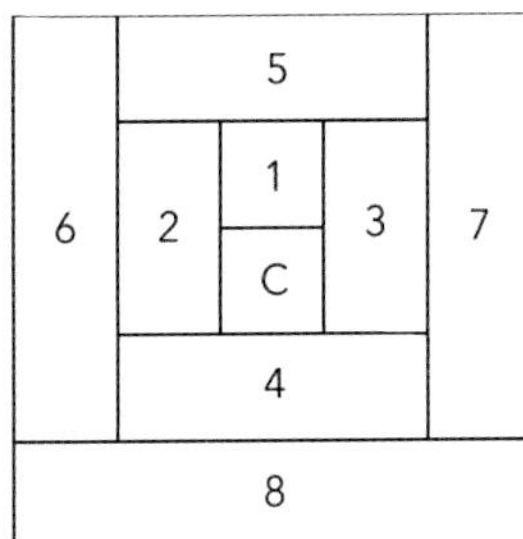

Top-sides-bottom

Quarter log cabin

Three-quarter log cabin

Top-sides-bottom: More of a logical possibility than a traditional piecing order – its inclusion here (and entirely unofficial name) might raise a few eyebrows. It consists of sewing a strip at the top of the block first, then to both sides, then the bottom.

Quarter log cabin: Sometimes known as a corner log cabin or half log cabin, it refers to a block where logs are sewn on two adjacent sides of the centre only.

Three-quarter log cabin: Less common, this is a block where logs are sewn on three sides of the centre.

LOCATING THE CENTRE

All log cabin blocks start with a centre, and when trying to figure out how a block was built it's a good idea to locate it first. It is sometimes obvious because it is a distinct colour, but sometimes not. In a traditional block, in which there are logs on four sides, the centre will be adjoined by four logs that in turn form a square (or a rectangle). In a quarter log cabin, the 'centre' will be in a corner and flanked by logs on two sides; in a three-quarter log cabin, it is a piece surrounded on three sides.

By looking at the block, you can then follow the way it has been pieced. The first log is going to be the same width as the centre; the second log flanks the centre and the first log; the third log flanks the centre and the second log; and the fourth log flanks the first log, the centre and the third log. In a courthouse steps block, there will be symmetry: the first two logs on opposite sides of the centre will have the same width as the centre, and the third and fourth logs sandwich the first log, the centre and the second log.

All this being said, it's worth bearing in mind that not all log cabin blocks will be pieced in a systematic way and some might therefore be more difficult to dissect.

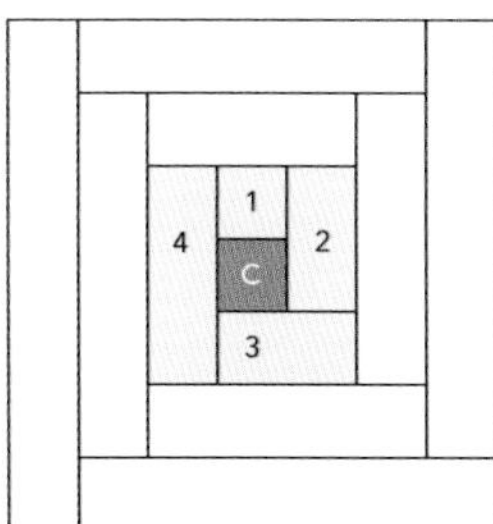

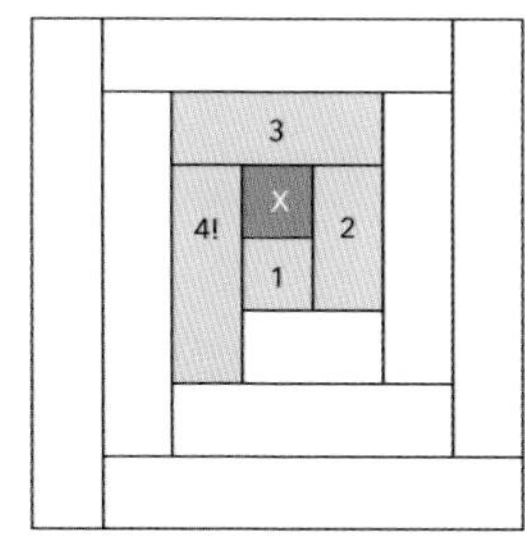

The first round of logs around the centre should make a square, as shown in the left-hand block. The square marked 'X' on the right-hand block cannot be the centre because the four logs surrounding it do not form a square.

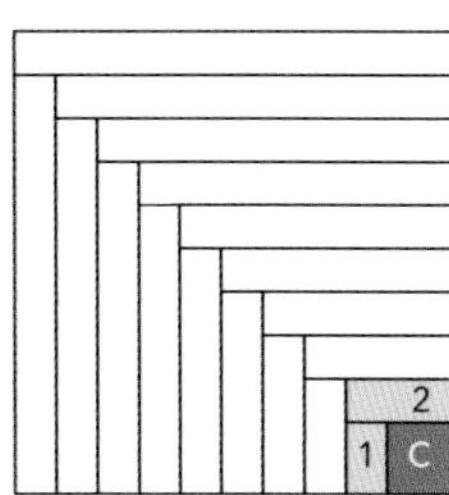

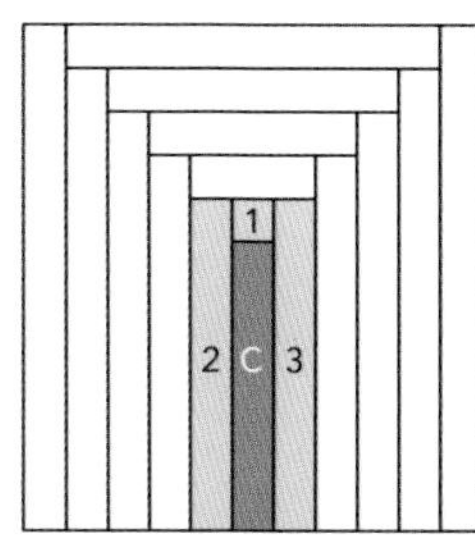

The centre of a quarter log cabin will be on a corner; in a three-quarter log cabin it will be flanked by logs on three sides.

TRADITIONAL PATTERNS AND HOUSETOP QUILTS

Traditionally, log cabin quilts were made of multiple square blocks which featured a light and dark side and a red centre. These blocks were then used to create a pattern within the quilt and, as with the variations within the blocks, the possibilities are infinite. Below are classic examples of log cabin quilt arrangements. Another form of log cabin quilt is the housetop, which consists of oversized log cabin blocks that cover the entire surface of the quilt. The Gee's Bend quilters have made stunning examples of housetop quilts, some with a single block, others with a 2 x 2 or 3 x 3 grid. An online search will bring up a wealth of examples, both of traditional block arrangements and housetop quilts.

Straight setting

Sunshine and shadows

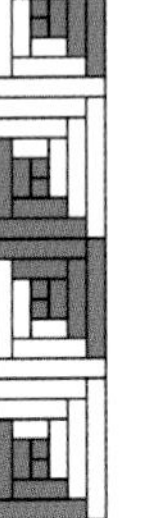

Fields and furrows

Chevron

PLANNING YOUR BLOCKS

Most of the blocks in this book I planned ahead using graph paper, where one square represents 1" x 1" (2.5 x 2.5cm). If you are planning to make blocks featuring various widths of strips, you can use graph paper with 1mm gradations, or quilters' graph paper with imperial measurements. The type of graph paper you use doesn't matter much as long as you are consistent when drawing your block.

Here are two ways to draw your blocks:

1. Start with the centre and build it outwards, adding logs in the same way you would when sewing it.
2. Draw the outline to represent your desired finished size, then draw the logs from the outer round all the way to the centre. The first log you draw will be the last one that is sewn in and will go from one side of the block to the other. This is the technique I used to draw some of the blocks with different widths of strips, as it allowed me to figure what size the centre needed to be for the block to be square in the end.

I used shading pencils to visualize how different contrasts would lead to various effects. If you would like to play around with multiple block arrangements, scan or take a photo of a block illustration in the Block Directory on pages 174–204, multiply the image, print it out, cut out the blocks and try out different configurations.

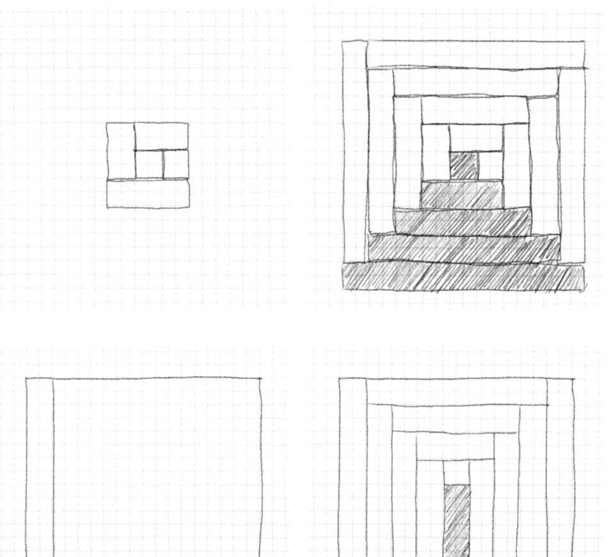

Starting with the centre, drawing logs as the block will be pieced.

Starting from a set size of block, drawing logs from the outside towards the centre.

BASIC SKILLS

CUTTING FABRIC

Rotary cutter method

Making log cabin blocks involves cutting a lot of strips of fabric, which is, on the whole, faster to do using a rotary cutter and a ruler than scissors. This technique works well for quilting cottons, woven cottons, denims and other relatively stable materials. Keep in mind that rotary blades can get blunt very quickly, depending on the type of fabric you are cutting and the quality of your cutting mat. If you find that you are struggling to get a clean cut after one pass, it might be time to put in a fresh blade.

To cut strips using a rotary cutter:

1. Line up your fabric on a cutting mat so the bulk lies on the side of your dominant hand.
2. If the edge of your piece of fabric is uneven, straighten it up by cutting out a thin strip using the rotary cutter and the ruler: while keeping the ruler firmly in place with your non-dominant hand, position your rotary cutter straight (upright) against the side of the ruler at the bottom of the fabric, and roll the blade firmly against the ruler, moving away from your body.

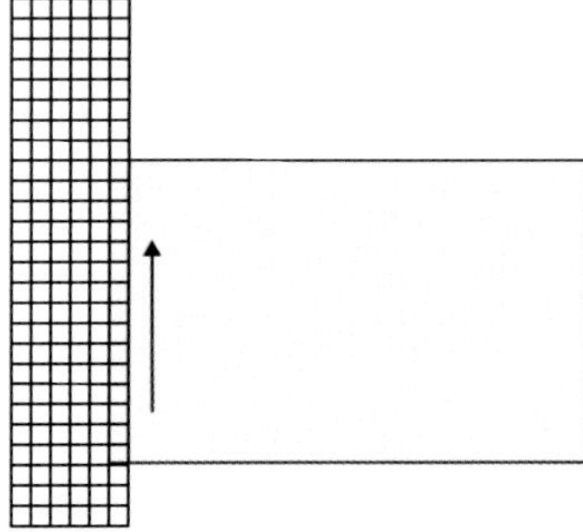

Cut, starting from the bottom of the fabric (right handed set up).

3. Before removing the length of fabric you have just cut, move the ruler and place it on top of the remaining fabric. This way, your carefully lined up fabric won't move.

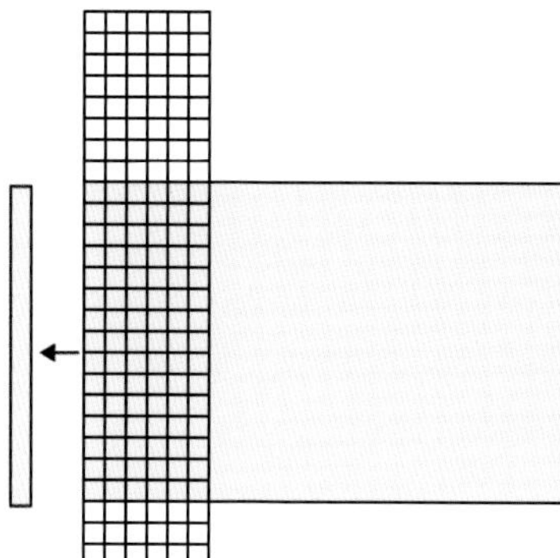

Move your ruler on top of your fabric to keep it in place.

4. Once you have a straight edge, you can start making your strips: position the ruler on top of your fabric, making sure the edge is straight and that the width of your strip is even and your measurement accurate.
5. Cut your first strip, then carry on.

If you are working with a wide piece of fabric, you can fold it in two and cut strips out of the folded piece, making sure the edges of both folded halves are lined up. I sometimes fold my fabric in three layers, but I would not recommend more than that, as it increases the chances of the strips being wobbly. If you are working with a small piece of fabric, you can create longer strips by sewing them end to end.

Thread pull method

While the rotary cutter method will work a charm with fabrics like quilting cotton – which tends to keep still under the ruler – linen, silk and fabrics with a lot of drape will be harder to cut straight: the fabric will look straight on the mat, but go wobbly as soon as you pick up a strip of fabric.

For linen, it helps to cut along the crosswise or lengthwise grain of the fabric (cutting parallel to the threads in a plain woven fabric). To do so, one trick is to cut the strips along the selvedge, which provides a straight edge that you can use to line up the fabric on the cutting mat. Alternatively, you can use the thread pull technique, which creates a straight edge that lines up with the grain of the fabric.

To cut strips using the thread pull technique:

1. Iron your fabric.
2. Lay the fabric on a flat surface and find the first thread that runs through the whole length of your piece (the edge is likely to be frayed and/or uneven from prior cutting).
3. Pick that thread out using a pin or the pointy end of a seam ripper.
4. Pull the thread gently, along the whole length of fabric. If the thread breaks, locate the broken end, pick the thread out and carry on pulling until you create a gap in the weave across the whole length of your piece.
5. Using scissors, cut slowly through the gap (doing this against a contrasting surface helps).

You can use this technique for cutting every strip of fabric, or use your ruler and rotary cutter to cut strips now that you have a straight edge.

Some fabrics will shift and wobble no matter what. For these you can use the thread pull method for each strip of fabric. For fabrics with no obvious thread to pull, like velvets or delicate silks, use a ruler and a tailor's chalk to mark a cutting line, then cut slowly with scissors when you are confident your mark is straight and the width of your strip of fabric is consistent throughout.

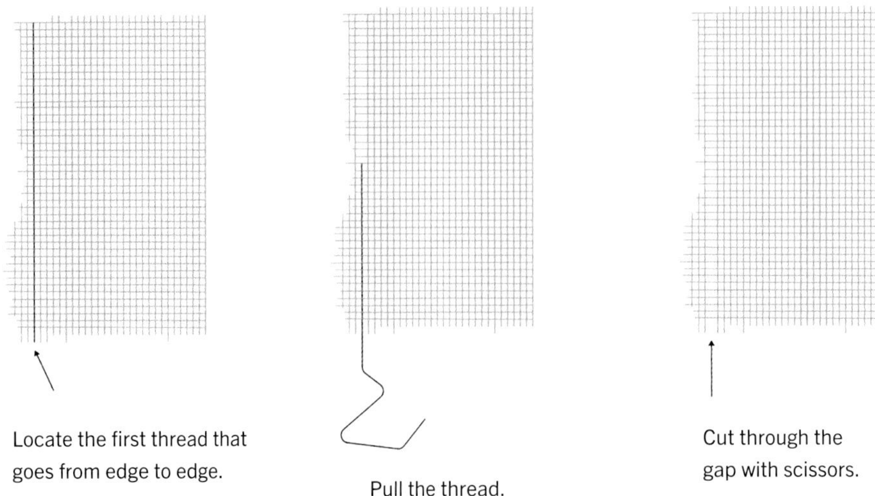

Locate the first thread that goes from edge to edge.

Pull the thread.

Cut through the gap with scissors.

SEAMS AND SEAM ALLOWANCES

Stitch length

The stitch length on your sewing machine refers to the distance between each stitch, either in millimetres or in stitches per inch. Your machine will have a default stitch length that it will revert to each time you switch it on. For some machines this is 2.5mm, for others it is 2.2mm. This default is fine for most tasks, but you might want to consider reducing it slightly for fabrics with a very loose weave in order to prevent the seam allowance from fraying and the seams from unravelling.

Backstitching

Backstitching consists of starting and finishing a seam by reversing the direction of stitch on your sewing machine and sewing over a few stitches to prevent the seam from coming undone. While necessary in clothes making, in patchwork seams are usually secured by the intersecting seam from the next piece of fabric that is added. This is the case for log cabin blocks, where seams are stitched over when the next log is added. If you are worried about this, or if you are making something with your block(s) that will have a lot of wear and tear, feel free to backstitch over every seam.

Seam allowance

The seam allowance is the area between the stitching line and the fabric edge, the extra fabric you need to sew two pieces together so that the seam won't unravel. Different fabrics call for different seam allowances, and fabrics that are prone to fraying benefit from a wider seam allowance.

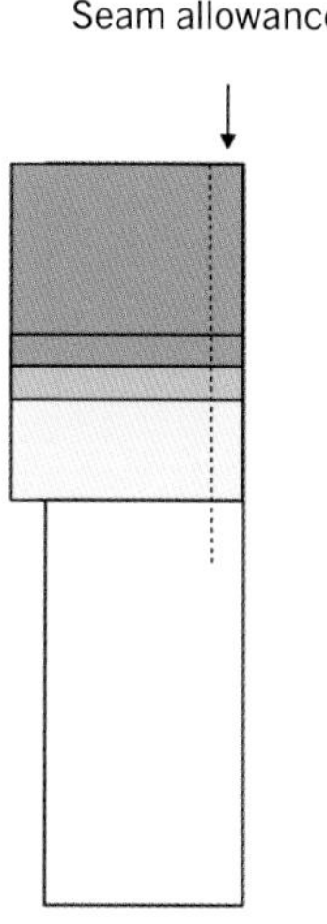

The common seam allowance in quilting is ¼" (about 0.6cm), narrower than the ⅝" (1.6cm) often used in clothes making. I find that it is wide enough for the type of linen that I use and have never had problems with seams coming undone, but some quilters recommend going up to ½" (1.3cm) when working with fabrics that have a looser weave. Feel free to add whichever seam allowance you are most comfortable with to the measurements listed in the Block Directory, which do not include the seam allowances.

There are various ways to keep a consistent seam allowance when stitching together pieces of fabric for patchwork. I find it easier to align the edge of the fabrics I am stitching together to the edge of the walking foot on my sewing machine. In order to achieve a ¼" (0.6cm) seam allowance I need to move my needle to the right slightly to adjust the space between my needle and the edge of the foot. Not all sewing machines will allow you to move the needle to the left or the right, so the space between your needle and the edge of the foot might be wider than a quarter inch. If this is the case, you have a few options:

1. You can adjust the seam allowance when you cut the fabric strips: just measure the distance between your needle and the right edge of your walking foot and adjust the width of your strips accordingly using this formula: **width of log + (seam allowance x 2) = width of strip to cut**
2. You can purchase a ¼" (0.6cm) walking foot compatible with your sewing machine.
3. You can mark your sewing machine by sticking a piece of masking tape ¼" (0.6cm) away from the needle, which you can then use as a guide when sewing.
4. Or you can decide not to worry about it and sew your strips as they come, with a wider seam allowance. The only place where you should be careful is when using very narrow strips (in the double line blocks for instance): a wider seam allowance will result in very skinny and potentially uneven lines, which may not be desirable.

In all cases, keep an eye on the edge of your pieces as you stitch to make sure that the piece underneath doesn't shift. If it shifts under, and your seam allowance becomes very narrow as a consequence, it is worth unpicking the seam and starting again. A seam allowance that is too narrow is likely to cause the seam to come undone. You can use pins to keep both strips together if you find that it helps.

IRONING/PRESSING YOUR SEAMS

Many quilting books and tutorials will urge you to 'press' your seams rather than 'ironing' them. Pressing a seam involves lowering your iron on one section of the seam, then lifting it up and lowering it on the next section of the seam. Ironing a seam involves lowering your iron at the beginning of the seam and then sliding it along the whole length of the seam without lifting it. The argument for pressing is that ironing can disturb the adjacent seams as well as stretch and distort the fabric. The argument against is that it is time consuming and a burn hazard when you try to keep a seam open before lowering your iron onto it. I use both techniques (I press small pieces and dense patchwork, but iron long seams) but feel free to use the technique you are most comfortable with. In this book I have used the words 'press' and 'iron' interchangeably.

There are two main ways to press your seams, and your choice will depend on the look you would like to achieve and your personal preference. My default is to press the seams open, as I prefer the flat surface it gives to a block. I press seams sideways when I want to add texture or if I am using very narrow logs.

Open

Pressing each seam open as you go, before sewing on the next strip of fabric. It gives a flat surface on the front of the piece. It can be done with an iron, a seam roller or your fingers (see tips overleaf).

To press your seams open: Open the seam with your finger then press it flat with your iron, then turn your block over and press the front.

Sideways

This involves pressing the seam allowance of both pieces of fabric towards one side of the block, typically outwards, away from the centre. It creates a little ridge on the front, and the thicker the fabric, the more visible the ridge will be. It can be done systematically, or used for a subtle effect on one or two sides of the log cabin (see for instance Blocks 40 and 92).

To press seams sideways: Starting on the back of your fabric, press both seam allowances to one side. Turn the block over and press the front, making sure that the fold is as close as possible to the seam. I sometimes iron my seams sideways from the front by nudging the newly sewn log outwards using the tip and the side of the iron.

Tips for pressing/ironing as you go

When sewing several strips of fabric to make a block, pressing each seam can quickly become tedious, especially if you have to get up and sit down each time. There are a few ways to make this more bearable:

Finger pressing: Press open the seam with your thumb on one side and your index on the other. It won't be perfectly flat but it will allow you to stitch on the next strip. At the end, you can press your seams flat with a hot iron, starting from the outer strips and working your way towards the middle of the block. If the block is an artwork and you like the texture, you can leave your piece as is (see Blocks 14, 17 and 98).

Using a seam roller: You can purchase a handy tool called a seam roller, and use it to press your seams directly on your working surface. Seam rollers are made of plastic or wood and are easily available online.

Using a mini-iron: Also available are mini-irons that you can use on a table top next to your sewing machine. You can make a small ironing surface by covering a wooden board with a few layers of heat resistant wadding/batting and a sturdy cotton top layer.

Changing your setup: Most ironing boards can be lowered, and if space allows you can install it next to your sewing machine and press as you go without getting up. Some techniques, like fabric foundation piecing, require you to press each seam before you sew the next piece on, so it's worth thinking about how to make your work station as ergonomic and efficient as possible.

BATCH PIECING

If you would like to make multiple iterations of the same block, it is worth organizing your strips of fabrics in advance and batch piecing the blocks. This means that rather than working on a single block from the centre out, you work on several blocks at the same time, one log at a time. For instance, if you want to make four blocks, you stitch the first log on each of the four centres before starting to sew the second log.

To batch piece four blocks:

1. Cut all your centres and enough fabric strips to make all your blocks.
2. Take the strip of fabric that corresponds to your first log and position one centre on top of it, right sides together.
3. Stitch the first centre to the strip of fabric, pausing just before you reach the end of that seam to position the second centre on the strip, without lifting the walking foot or cutting the thread.
4. Carry on sewing, pausing to add the third centre, and then the fourth.
5. Remove the sewn strip from the machine.
6. Cut each piece apart with scissors or your ruler and rotary cutter and press your seams open or sideways.
7. Repeat the operation with the second log, then the third, etc.

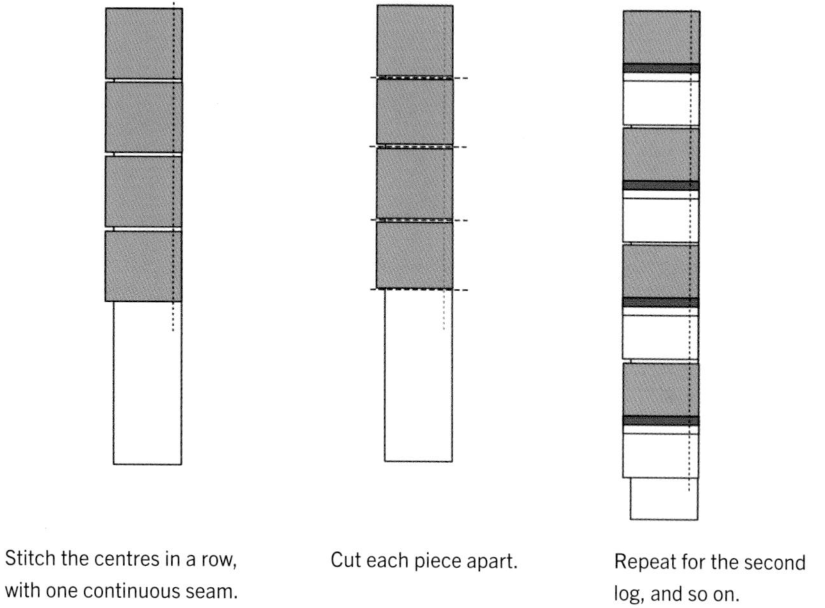

Stitch the centres in a row, with one continuous seam.

Cut each piece apart.

Repeat for the second log, and so on.

Note: You can leave a few millimetres between each centre/block on your strip of fabric, and press your seams before cutting the blocks apart, whichever works best for you and the type of fabric you use. I find that sometimes linen shifts sideways, which results in a wonky cut, so if I am looking for accuracy I will press the seam first then cut the blocks apart with a ruler and a rotary cutter.

HOW TO SEW A LOG CABIN BLOCK

This section walks you through the steps of making a traditional log cabin block. If you have never sewn one before, start here. We will cover two methods: the basic method, which involves sewing your strips of fabric directly onto your centre, one log at a time, and the fabric foundation piecing method, which involves sewing the pieces of your block onto a backing fabric. While I used the first one for the majority of the blocks in this book, the second one is a useful technique to know when working with delicate or stretchy fabrics.

Both methods are easy to master, and the underlying principle is the same:

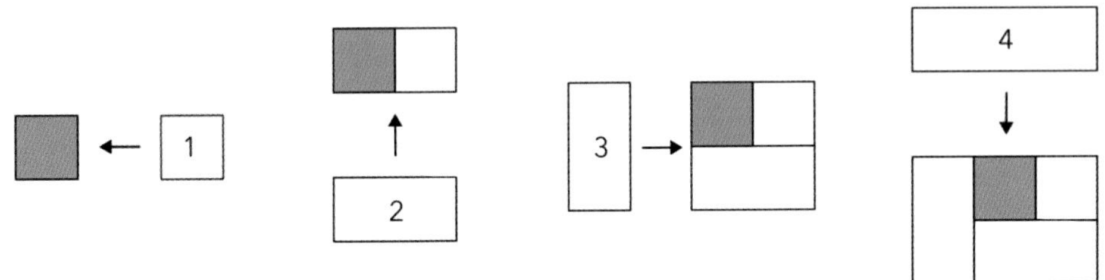

Logs are sewn, in order, onto the centre.

Focusing on the first round is crucial, but, once you have sewn the first four logs, there's an easy way to find out where the next log goes: it will always be on the side where one log is bookended by the end of two other logs. In other words, just look for the side with three pieces of fabric and that is where you are going to add your next log. In courthouse steps blocks, you will find that there are two sides like this; these are where your next two logs go.

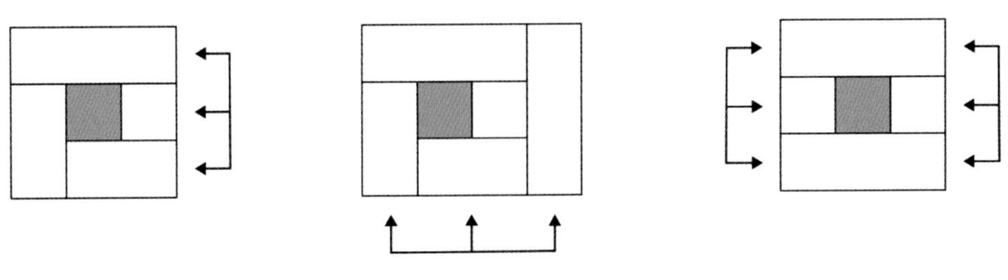

The fifth log will go on the side where there are three pieces of fabric.

And so on.

In a courthouse steps block, where blocks are sewn in pairs, the next two logs will be on opposite sides.

BASIC METHOD

1. Cut the centre and your strips of fabric. You do not need to pre-cut your logs. Note that if your fabrics have a front and a back (most prints do), the front of your centre needs to be against the front of the strip.
2. Position your centre on top of the first strip of fabric, lining up the top and right edges (pins are optional).

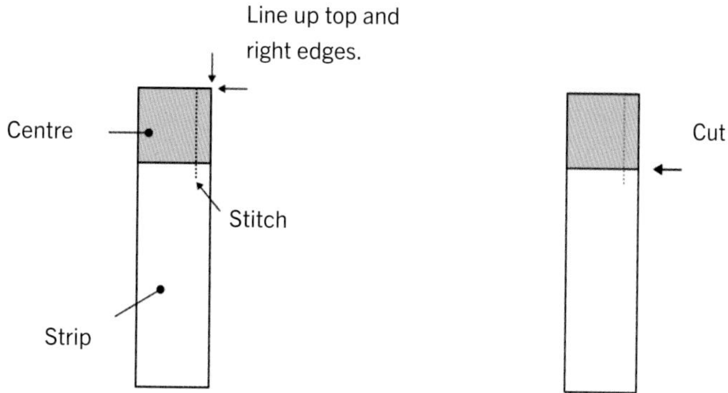

3. Stitch the centre onto the strip.
4. Trim the strip of fabric so that its edges are flush with the edges of the centre. Open the block and press the seam.
5. Rotate the block and position it on top of the next strip, top and right edges aligned, so that the back of the block is facing up.
6. Stitch both pieces together.
7. Cut the strip, open the block, press the seam, and carry on with the following logs.

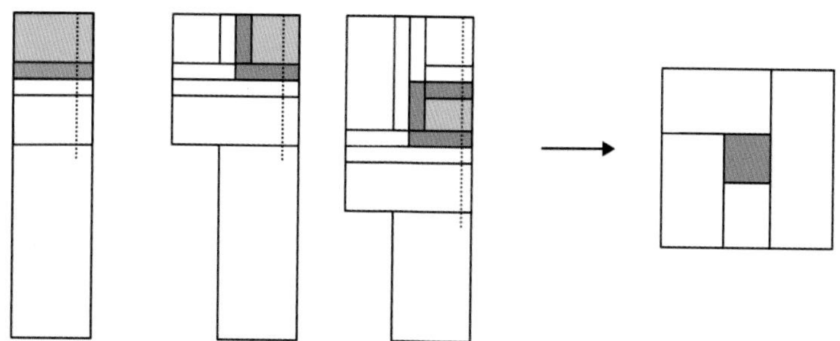

Carry on with the following logs.

Clockwise or anticlockwise?

For the times when the order of piecing matters, it's worth keeping in mind:

- The order of piecing when looking at the back of the block is opposite to the order when looking at the front of the block: from the back, a clockwise block will be pieced anticlockwise, and vice versa.
- When you place your block, right side down, on your strip of fabric for sewing the second log, the centre needs to be at the top for a clockwise block, and at the bottom for an anticlockwise block.

FABRIC FOUNDATION PIECING

Fabric foundation piecing involves sewing each patchwork piece onto a backing fabric. It is a very useful technique when working with delicate fabrics like silk or stretchy material like jersey, as the backing fabric stabilizes the patchwork and minimizes the stretch and pull on the seams. Fabric foundation pieced blocks are ready to use and do not require a backing or quilting stitches, as the foundation fabric provides the backing and the raw edges are enclosed between it and the top patchwork. It is excellent if you wish to make a quick cushion, for instance.

Foundation piecing involves what is known as the 'stitch and flip' method: the first piece (the centre) is pinned onto the foundation fabric, the first log is sewn onto both the centre and the foundation fabric, then the log is 'flipped' open and ironed flat.

Choosing fabric for foundation piecing

Your foundation fabric can be any light to medium weight cotton that doesn't stretch. I use quilting cotton remnants, but a light or medium weight calico cotton (known as muslin in the US) is excellent for this. Choose a fabric that won't show through your patchwork, and prewash it to avoid any shrinking. To make a fabric foundation pieced block:

1. Cut a piece of foundation fabric so that it is about 1" (2.5cm) bigger in every direction than the final block dimension. Cut your strips of fabric and centre as you would for a basic block, with a ¼" (0.6cm) seam allowance.
2. Position your centre on your backing fabric, right side facing up, and pin it in place.
3. For your first log, measure the width of your centre and cut this length from your strip of fabric.

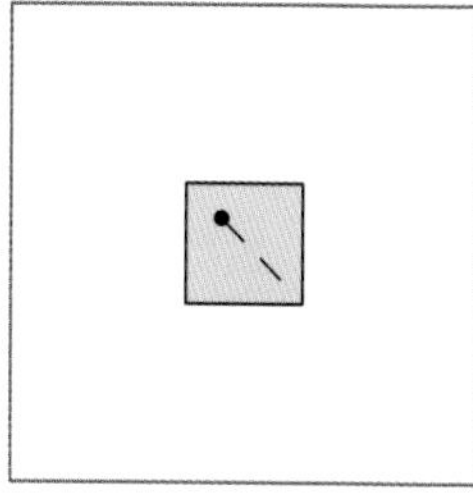
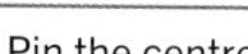

Pin the centre.

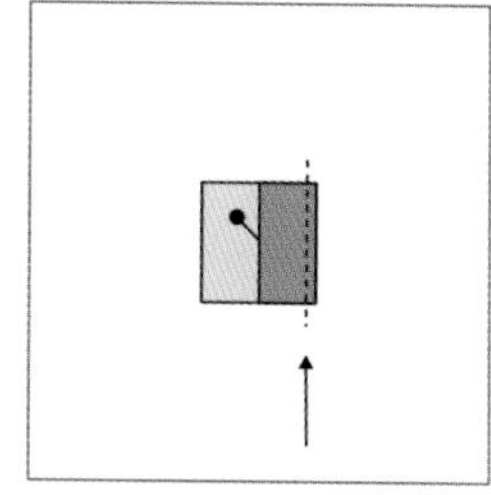

Stitch first log.

4. Position this first strip on top of the centre, right side facing down, lining the edge of the log with the edge of the centre.
5. Stitch along the edge of the log with a ¼" (0.6cm) seam allowance, going through all the layers (log, centre, foundation fabric).
6. Flip the log outwards and iron it flat, making sure that your fold is as close as possible to the stitch line.
7. Measure the width of the next log, cut it from your strip, place it on the second side of your centre, stitch, flip and iron.
8. Carry on around the centre until you have covered the surface of your foundation.

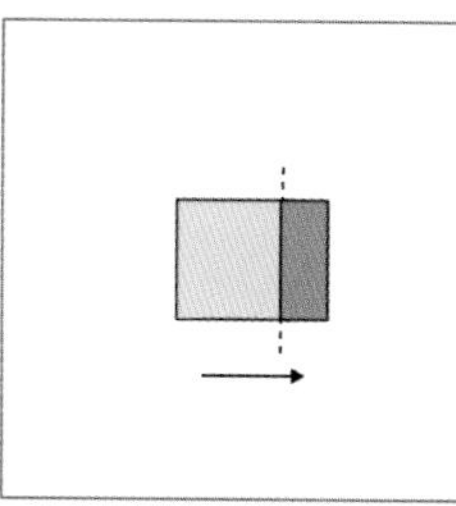

Iron outwards.

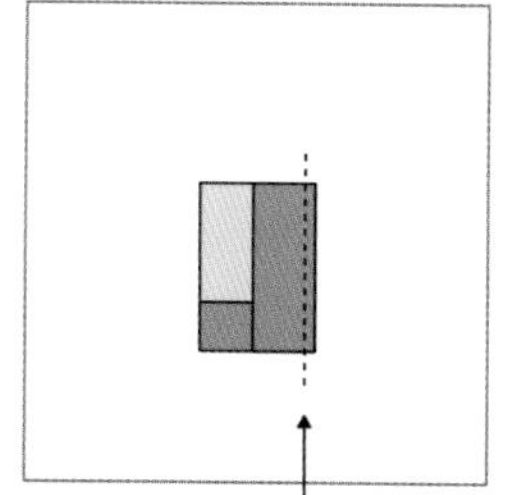

Rotate and stitch second log.

9. Trim your block down to the desired size.

Things to remember:

- Depending on where you positioned the centre of your block and the width of your logs, it's possible that you will reach the edge of your foundation fabric on one side but not the others. You can stop there and trim the excess foundation fabric, or continue filling the space with more logs on the empty sides only.

- Make sure that your log is ironed as flat as possible before sewing the next one. Because the logs are sewn on the foundation fabric, there's nowhere for excess fabric to go and logs that haven't been ironed flat can end up bulging slightly.

VARIATIONS

PIECED CENTRES

The log cabin is a block in itself but also a good technique to use when you want to frame a beloved piece of fabric, or another patchwork block. You often find in antique quilts, for instance, that the centre of a log cabin is pre-pieced, from simple half square triangles to complex star designs. Here are a few for you to try.

HALF SQUARE TRIANGLE CENTRE

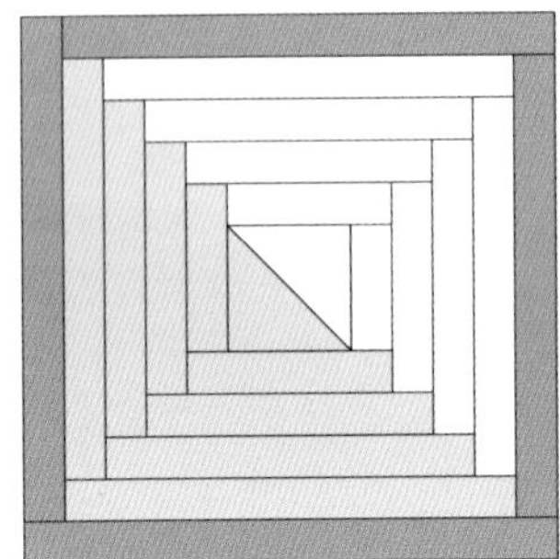

To make two half square triangle centres (see page 156 if you need eight):

1. Cut one square from each of your two fabrics using this formula for the measurements, which includes a ¼" (0.6cm) seam allowance and a bit of extra so that you can square it down to size:
   finished size + 1" (2.5cm)
2. Lay one square on top of the other.
3. Using a ruler and a fabric marker, trace a diagonal line from one corner to the opposite corner.
4. Using a ¼" (0.6cm) seam allowance, stitch on both sides of the diagonal.
5. Cut on the diagonal line you marked in step 3, press the seams and trim your squares down to your exact measurements.

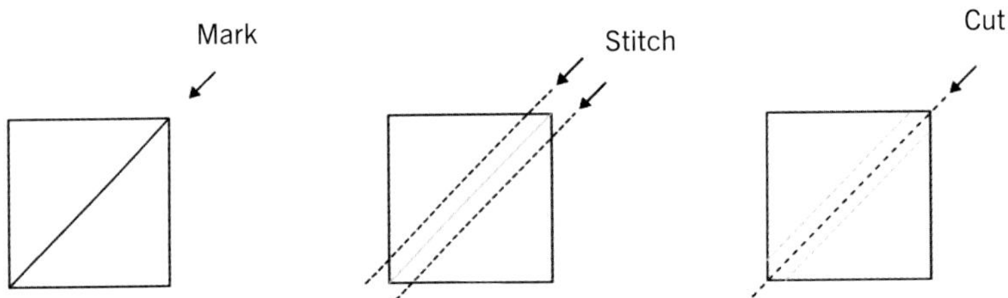

QUARTER SQUARE TRIANGLE CENTRE

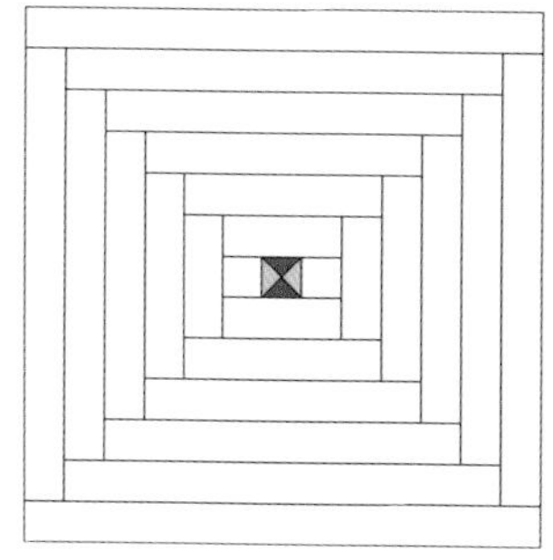

The centre of Block 22 consists of a square made of four equal size triangles. To make two quarter square triangle blocks with a ¼" (0.6cm) seam allowance and a bit of extra so that you can square it down to size:

1. Cut one square from each of your two fabrics using this formula for the measurements: **finished size + 1½" (3.8cm)**
2. Make two half square triangle blocks as instructed in the previous section. Press your seams sideways, towards the same fabric for both blocks.
3. Layer the two blocks, so that each triangle faces the triangle in the contrasting fabric. Make sure your seams and edges are lined up; secure the two layers with a pin if you wish.
4. Using a ruler and a fabric marker, trace a diagonal line, going from one corner to the opposite corner and crossing the stitch line.

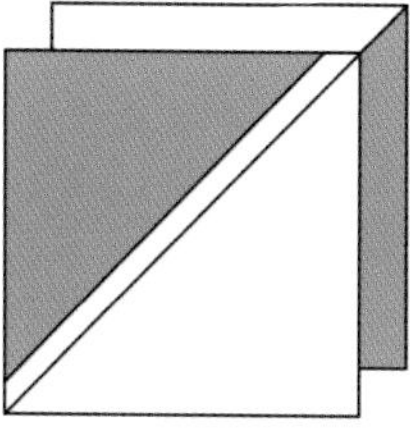

Layer the two blocks so that opposite colours face each other.

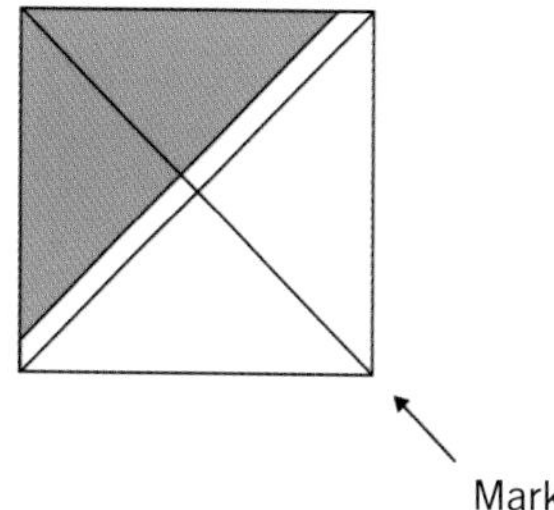

5. Using a ¼" (0.6cm) seam allowance, stitch on both sides of the diagonal.
6. Cut on the diagonal line you marked in step 4, press the seams and trim your squares down to size.

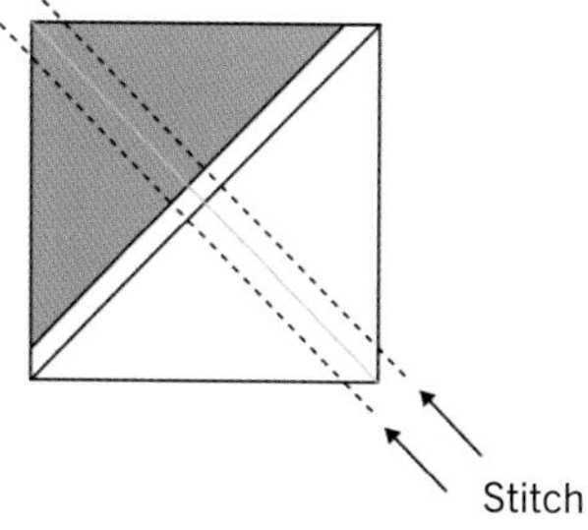

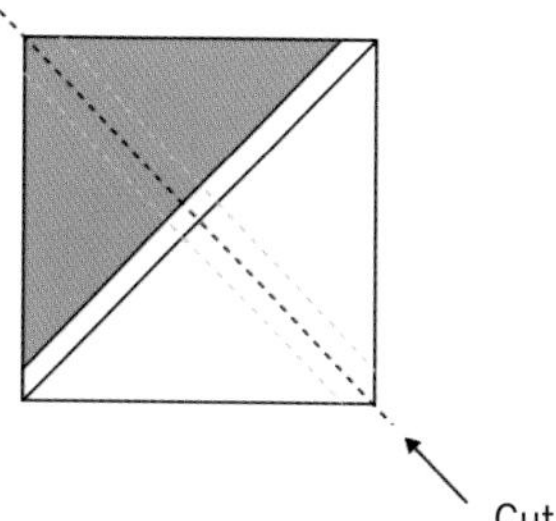

STRIPE CENTRE

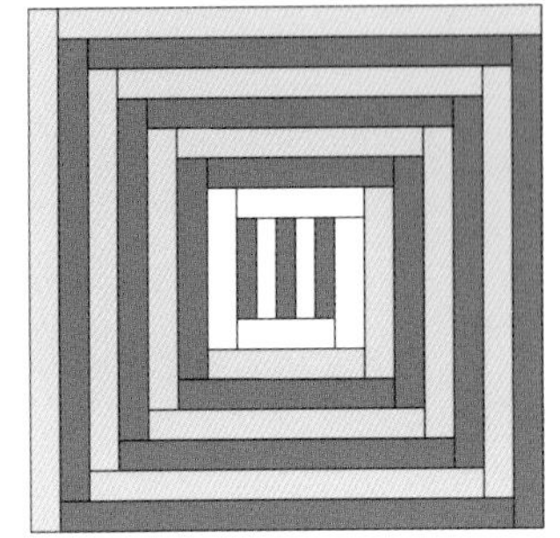

To make a striped centre like the one in Block 20, measuring 2½" x 2½" (6.4 x 6.4cm), plus a ¼" (0.6cm) seam allowance:

1. Cut two 1" (2.5cm) strips of fabric in different colours.
2. From these strips, cut three 3¼" (8.3cm) lengths from one colour and two 3¼" (8.3cm) lengths from the other colour.
3. Stitch these cut strips together, alternating the colours.

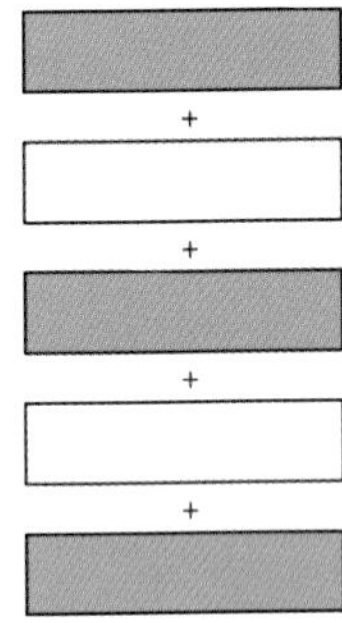

Join five strips in alternating colours.

4. Trim down to 3" x 3" (7.6 x 7.6cm).

CHECKERBOARD CENTRE

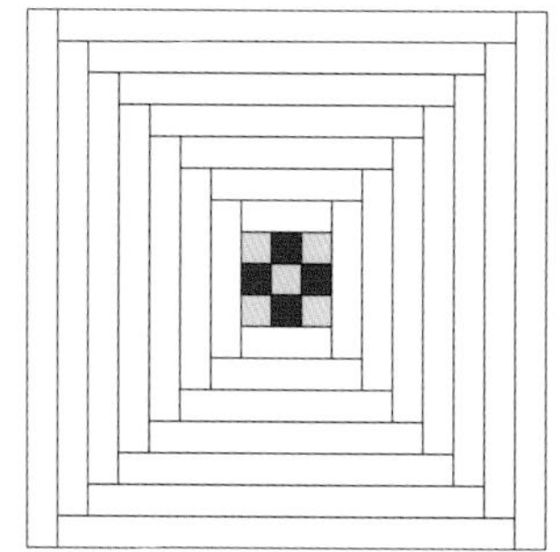

To make a checkerboard centre like the one in Block 21 (which looks like the beginning of a block with cornerstones), measuring 2¼" x 2¼" (5.7 x 5.7cm), plus a ¼" (0.6cm) seam allowance:

1. Cut nine 1¼" x 1¼" (3.2 x 3.2cm) squares, five of one colour, four of the other.
2. Stitch three rows of three squares in alternating colours.

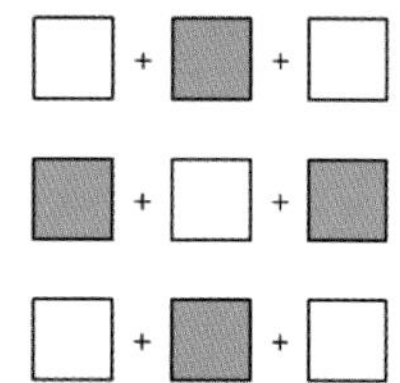

Create three rows of squares.

3. Stitch these three rows together, making sure the seams are lined up.

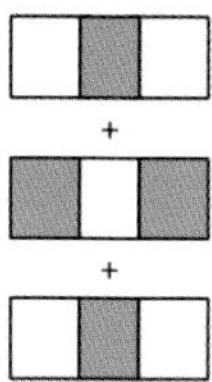

Join the three rows together.

CORNERSTONES

Cornerstones are little squares of contrasting fabric that are used to add a bit of interest to a quilt. In log cabin quilts, they are added to the end of logs to create a pattern within the block and/or across multiple blocks. They can be used to create an 'X' design on the square, a single diagonal line, as a small detail in one corner or be used across several blocks to create a design or emphasize the structure of a block. Cornerstones can be of the same size and colour as the centre, made of contrasting fabric, or even pre-pieced.

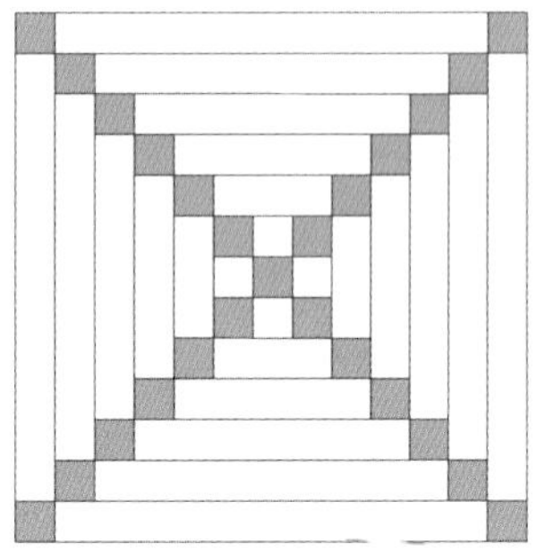
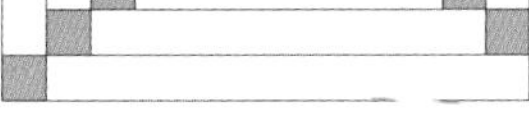

X

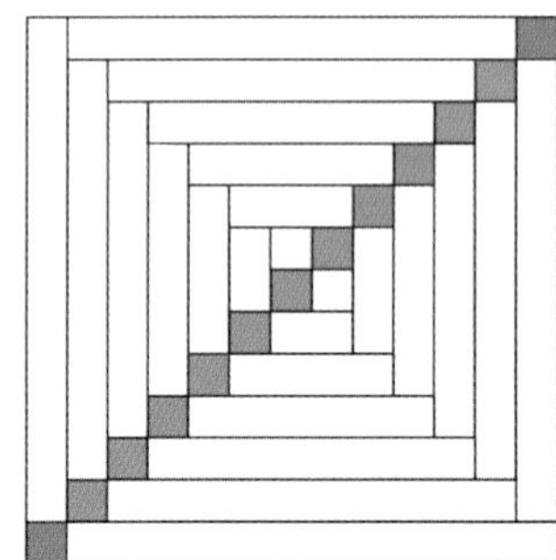

Diagonal

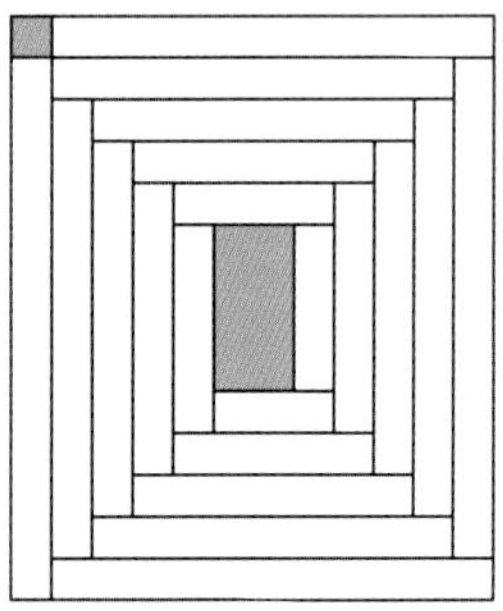

Single cornerstone

Multi-block design

PRE-CUT CORNERSTONES

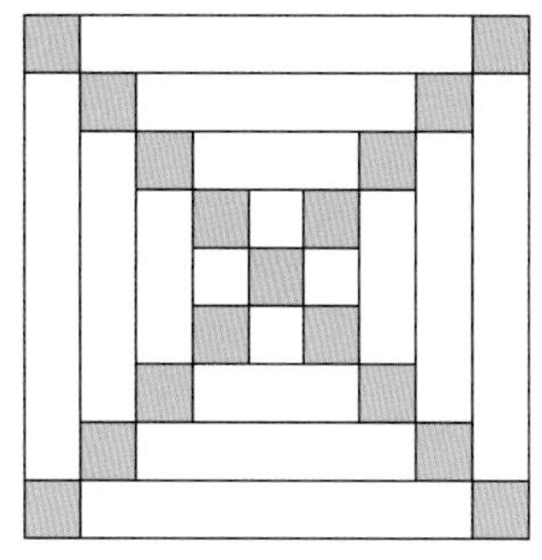

The most common form of cornerstone is a pre-cut square that is added at the end of a log, or two cornerstones that bookend a log. A block with an 'X' in cornerstones can be pieced clockwise or anticlockwise or as a courthouse steps block. Both blocks will look identical, so it is down to your own preference.

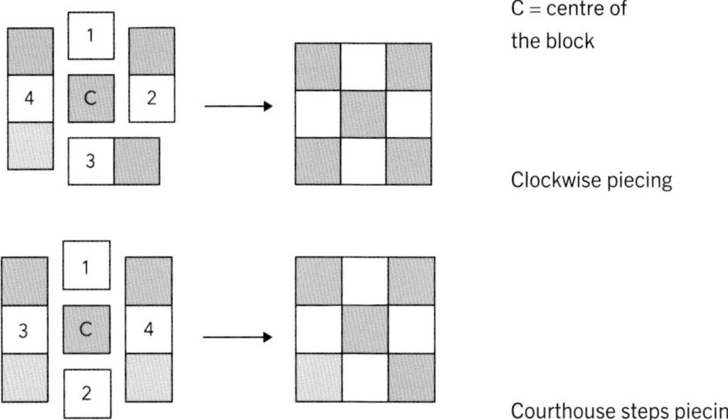

C = centre of the block

Clockwise piecing

Courthouse steps piecing

To add a log with one pre-cut square cornerstone:

1. Pre-cut your square cornerstones so they are the same width as the strip of fabric you want to add them to.
2. Sew the cornerstone at the top of the strip of fabric you want to use as a log (stitch on the short end). Press the seam.
3. Place your strip with the cornerstone on top of your block so that the seams are lined up. Pin in place if you wish.
4. Stitch, press the seam and cut the log in line with the side of the block.

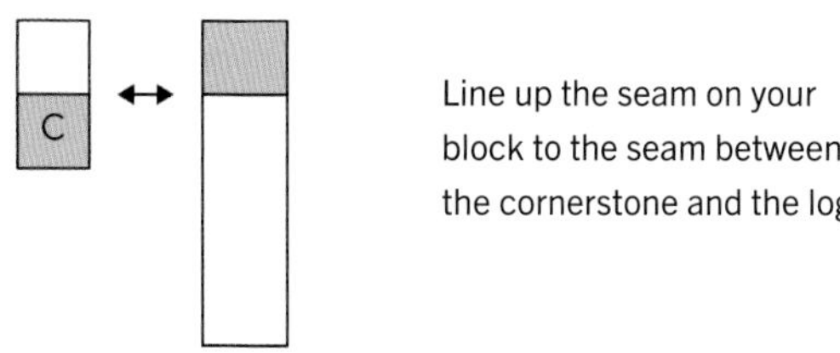

Line up the seam on your block to the seam between the cornerstone and the log.

To add a log with two pre-cut cornerstones:

1. When you reach the point of needing to add a log with two cornerstones, measure the width of the central piece of fabric (which may include cornerstones from the previous round, see image below), add your seam allowance, and then cut a strip of that length from your log fabric strip.
2. Bookend your log strip with two cornerstones. Press the seams.

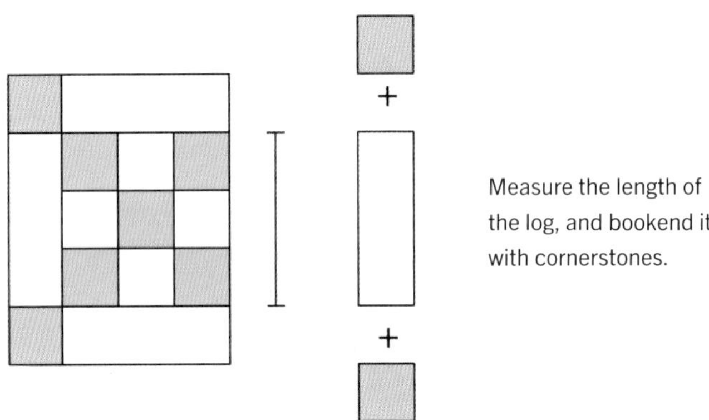

Measure the length of the log, and bookend it with cornerstones.

3. Line up your log with cornerstones on your block, so that the seams joining the log and the cornerstones are lined up against the seams of your block.

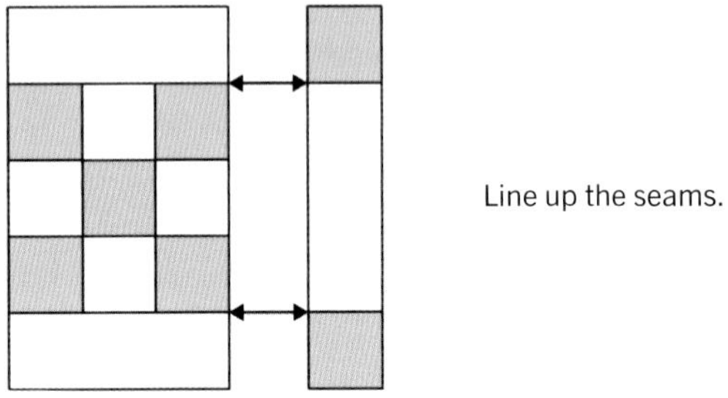

Line up the seams.

4. Stitch in place and press the seam.

OVERLAPPING CORNERSTONES

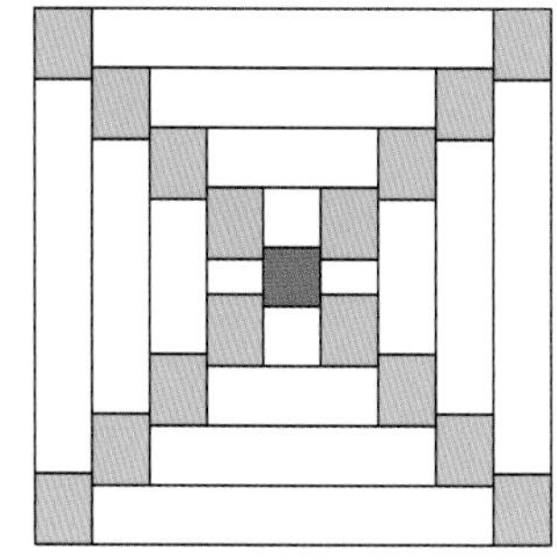

Less traditional are overlapping cornerstones, which, as the name suggests, overlap from one round to the next. For this method, you will have to cut your cornerstones as you go. You can also use scraps of fabric for this, as I did with Block 75.

To add a log with one overlapping cornerstone:

1. Cut a strip from your cornerstone fabric, the same width as the strip for your logs.
2. Sew the cornerstone strip at the end of the log strip (stitch on the short end). Press the seam.
3. Line up your strip on top of your block, so that the new cornerstone overlaps with the adjacent cornerstone (the seams will be offset).
4. Stitch in place, press the seam and trim at both ends.
5. Repeat step 2 for each new cornerstone.

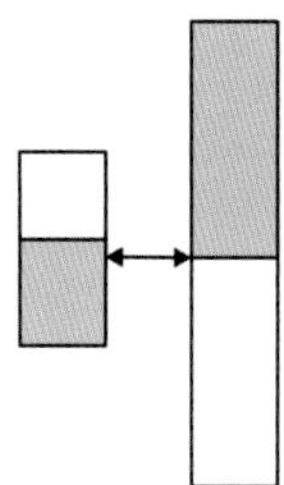

Offset the seams so that the cornerstones overlap.

To add two overlapping cornerstones:

1. Prepare two strips of your cornerstone fabric, the same width as the strip for your logs. You can cut your cornerstone strip in two, or estimate the length you will need and pre-cut that.
2. When you get to the point of adding a log with two cornerstones, measure the width of the central piece of fabric and cut a log of exactly that length or slightly shorter, without adding a seam allowance. You can eyeball your measurements if you would like your cornerstones to be uneven sizes.
3. Bookend your pre-cut log with cornerstone strips.
4. Line up your log with the cornerstone strip on top of your block, so that the cornerstones overlap with the adjacent cornerstones.
5. Stitch in place, press the seam and trim at both ends, cutting the cornerstones flush against the sides of the block.

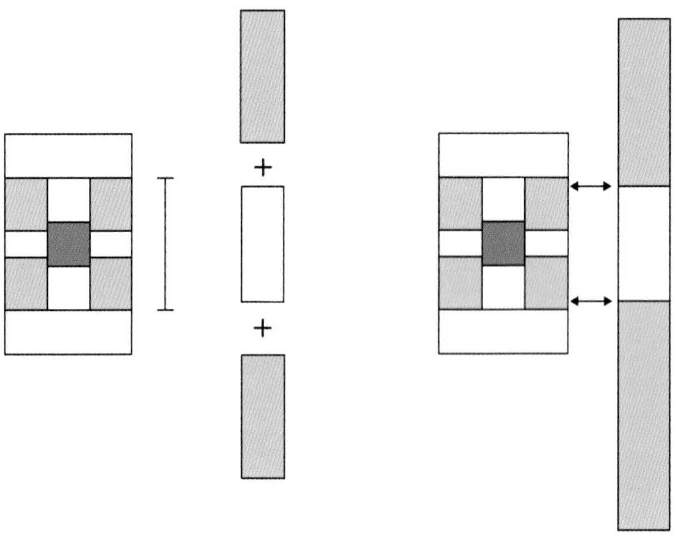

Measure the length of the log, and bookend it with cornerstone strips.

Line up your strip so that the cornerstones overlap with the ones from the previous round.

TRIANGLE CORNERSTONES

Unlike the square cornerstones, the triangle cornerstones in Block 27 are only added after a full round of logs are sewn on.

1. Count the number of triangle cornerstones you will need. For each cornerstone, cut a square of the same width as the strip for your logs (**log width** + **seam allowance**).
2. Stitch the first round of logs, as you would for a basic log cabin block (either in a courthouse steps pattern, like Block 27, or clockwise, like the example below).
3. Overlay a square of fabric on a corner of your block, making sure that both edges are lined up.
4. Stitch from one corner to the other (you can use a ruler and a fabric marker to draw a straight line first).

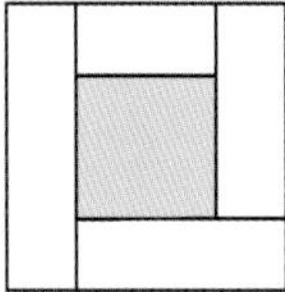

Add the first round of logs.

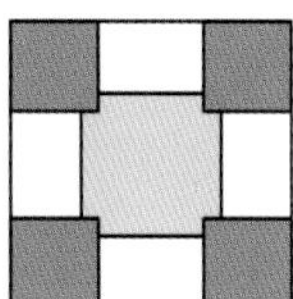

Line up the squares of fabric with the corners.

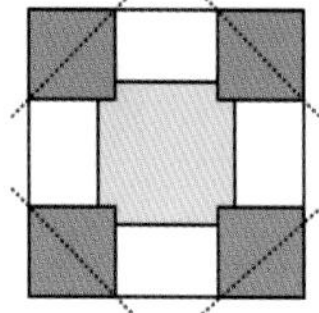

Stitch diagonally across the square.

5. Cut the corner ¼" (0.6cm) away from the seam and iron the cornerstone outwards.
6. Repeat for the three remaining cornerstones, and again for each round.

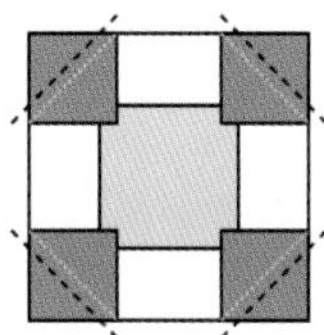

Trim the seam allowance.

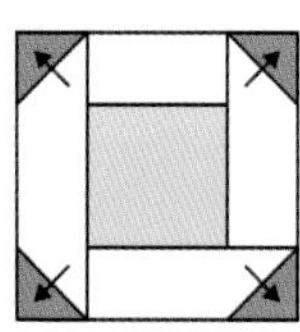

Iron the corners out.

HALF SQUARE TRIANGLE CORNERSTONES

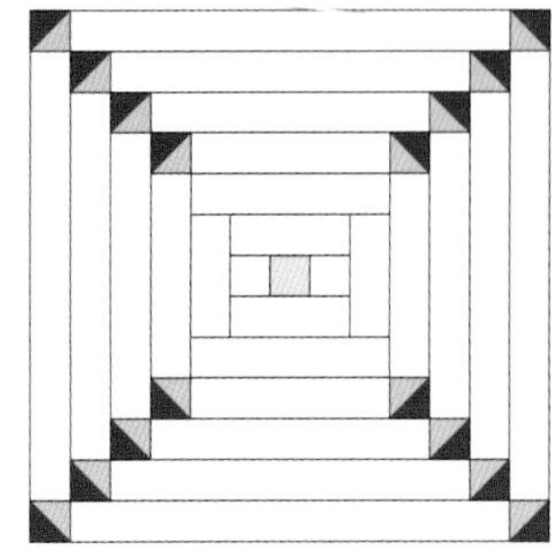

To make eight half square triangle blocks with a ¼" (0.6cm) seam allowance and a bit of extra so you can square it down to size:

1. Cut one square from each of your two fabrics using this formula: **(finished size + 1¼"/3.2cm) x 2**
2. Lay one square on top of the other, and, with a fabric marker and a ruler, draw lines joining each pair of opposing corners, making an 'X'.

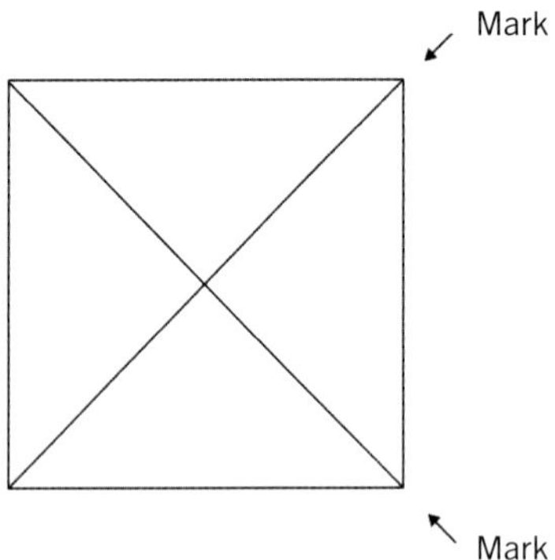

3. Using a ¼" (0.6cm) seam allowance, stitch on both sides of both diagonals.
4. Using your ruler and rotary cutter, cut on the lines you marked in step 2, then cut across each triangle as shown. Press the seams and trim your squares down to your exact measurements.

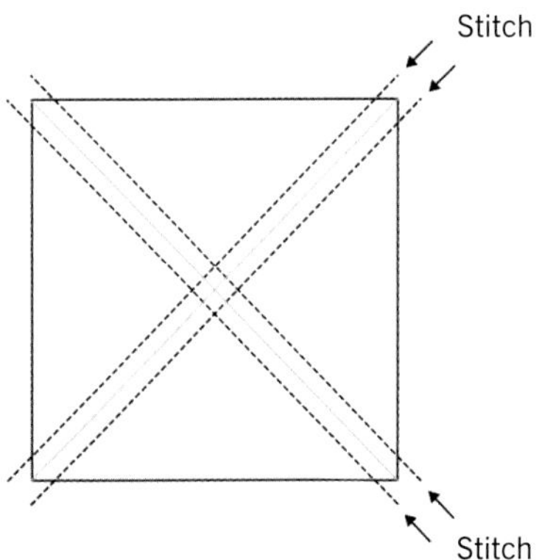

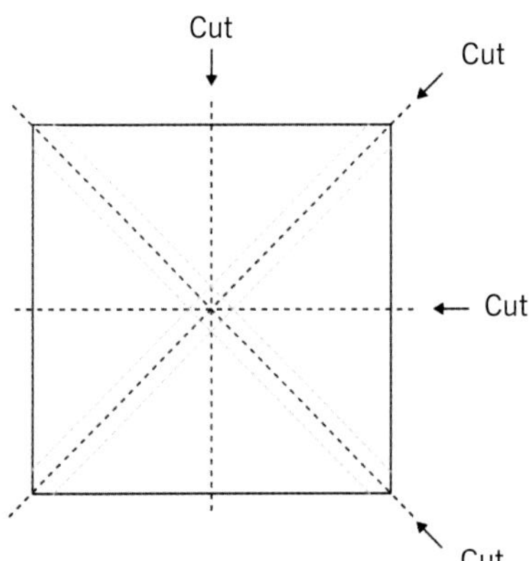

DOUBLE LINE AND STRIPE EFFECT BLOCKS

This variation is achieved by pre-piecing logs with two (or three) strips of fabric. The strips can be any width, but the combination of a narrow strip and a wide one can be particularly effective.

When it comes to piecing your block, the position of the narrow line will impact the overall look quite dramatically: positioning the narrow strip towards the centre of the block will create a boxy, almost architectural look, whereas positioning the wide strip towards the centre will achieve a more deconstructed look, with the dominant background colour being broken up by concentric thin lines. It's useful to play around with your strips before you start, and try different compositions.

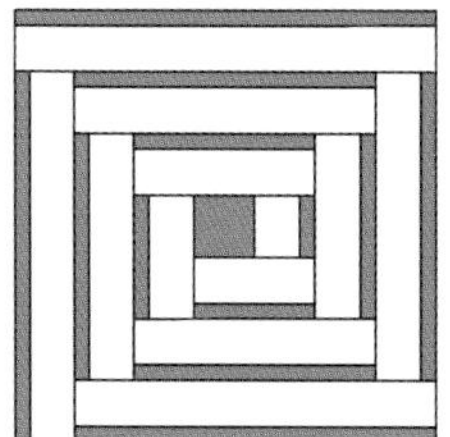

Thin lines outwards.

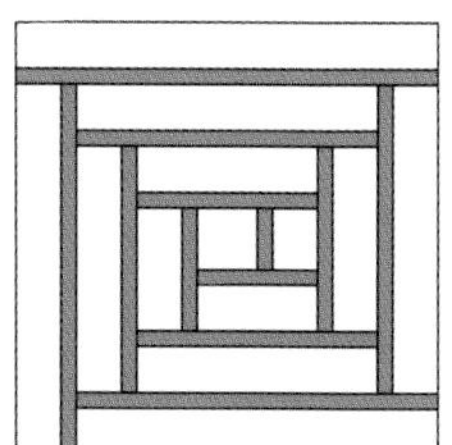

Thin lines inwards.

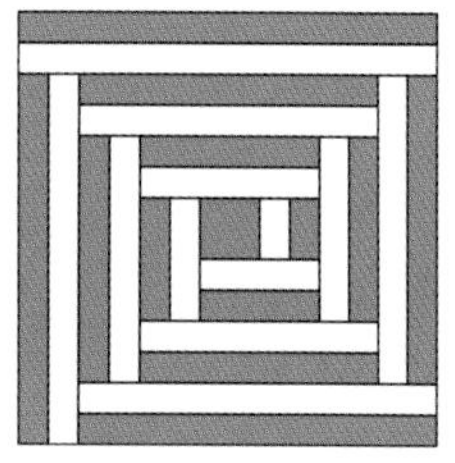

Double line with equal width strips.

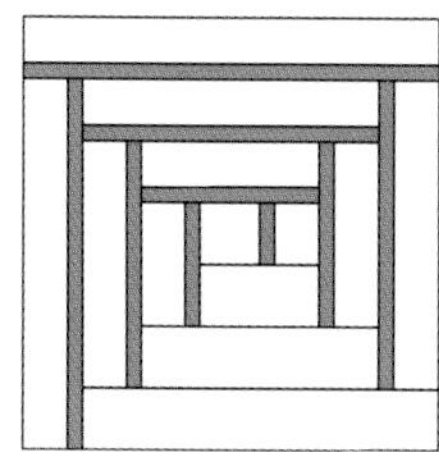

Double line block with plain logs.

DOUBLE LINE

To prepare double strips:

1. Cut two long strips of fabric, or piece smaller lengths by joining them end to end to create two long strips of roughly equal length (in this case iron the seams between strips open to have a smooth surface).
2. Place both strips right side against right side and stitch along the long edge.
3. Iron the seam sideways towards the wide side (otherwise the seam allowance will be in the way when you stitch the next log).
4. Use this strip for the logs of your block.

WONKY DOUBLE LINE

To make Block 32, you need to create logs that are pre-pieced one by one rather than in a continuous strip. To make 2" (5.1cm) wide strips (which give you 1½" (3.8cm) wide logs + ¼" (0.6cm) seam allowance):

1. Cut two 1¾" (4.4cm) strips of fabric in different colours.
2. Measure the length of your next log on the block (the width of the block), add 1" (2.5cm), and cut the resulting length from each strip.
3. Overlap your two strips so they are slightly askew, then stitch them together by following the edge of the strip on top. Trim the excess seam allowance.
4. Press the seam, then trim your strip so the long sides are parallel and the strip measures 2" (5.1cm) wide.
5. Sew it to your centre, trim the ends flush with the sides and repeat for each log.

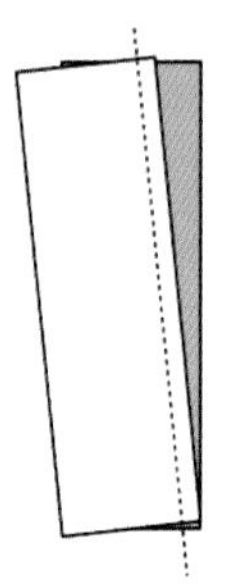

Stitch the top strip to the bottom.

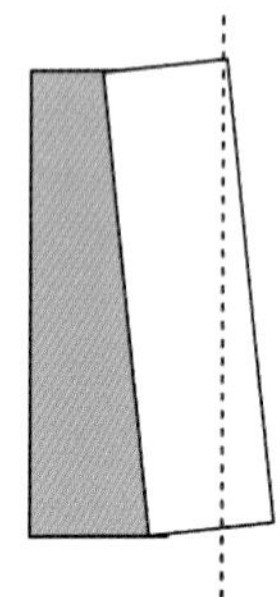

Trim your block so the long sides are parallel.

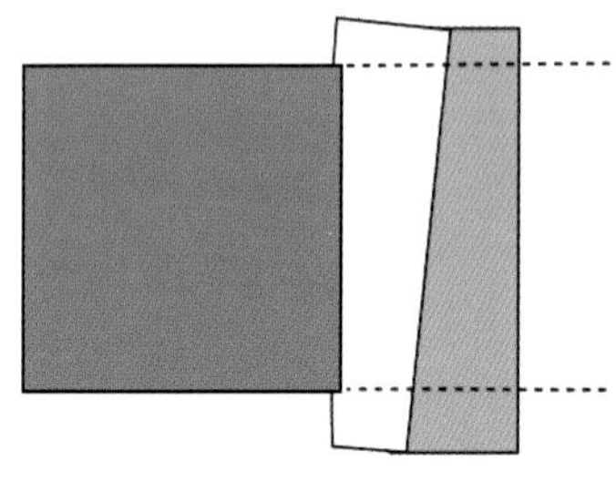

Stitch the log on your block and trim the ends.

TRIPLE LINE

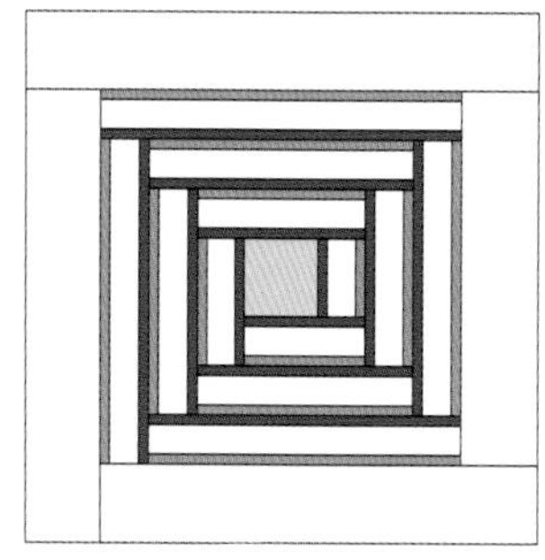

For triple line blocks, follow the same instructions but add one extra strip of fabric to the first two. You can play around by having equal width strips, narrow + wide + narrow strips, or narrow + narrow + wide strips.

SLASHED LOG CABIN

The inspiration for Block 33 comes from a block made by a participant in one of my log cabin workshops. The narrow strips of her double line block were on the very narrow end of the scale, and a bit wonky, which resulted in them barely showing up in the block. It looked like the block had been slashed with a sharp blade, hence the name. It was surprising and stunning all at once, and I knew some version of it had to feature here.

To make this block, proceed as you would for the basic double line block on page 157, but cut your narrow strip a little bit narrower and don't worry if it's uneven (you can use narrow scraps of fabric left from previous projects). I find that an irregular ⅝" (1.6cm), including seam allowance, works well. Pre-piece your strips of fabric as you would for a double line block, ironing the seam allowance towards the wider strip of fabric. When sewing the block, don't aim for a perfectly straight seam, and don't worry if you are sewing very close to the adjacent stitch line. You only want a sliver of fabric showing on the front. Iron your seam sideways towards the wider strip of fabric.

GREEK KEY

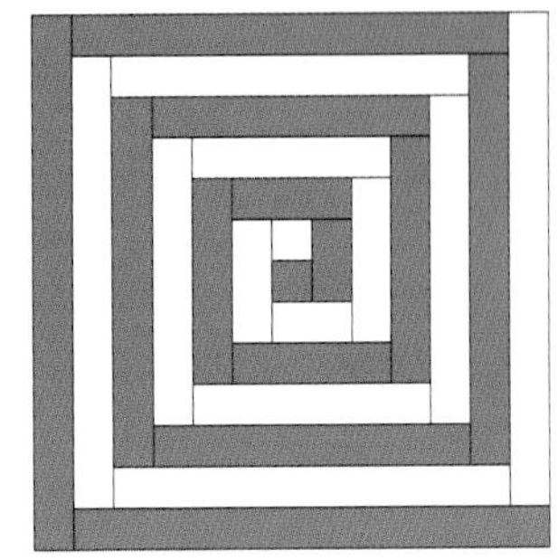

Not technically a double line log cabin block, the Greek Key block (Block 35) has nevertheless a pleasing effect of contrasting colours. It requires a bit of thinking, but it's a simple log cabin block, with logs being sewn clockwise or anticlockwise. The one thing that is counterintuitive is the order of the colours, especially as your piecing order will be the opposite of the direction of the design: to have a Greek key that goes clockwise, you will need to piece your block anticlockwise.

There's an easy formula to apply. For a block made of two colours, A and B, add logs following this order of colours:

- Centre: A
- Round 1: B, A, B, B
- Round 2: A, B, A, A
- Round 3: B, A, B, B
- Repeat rounds 2 and 3 until you have reached the desired size.

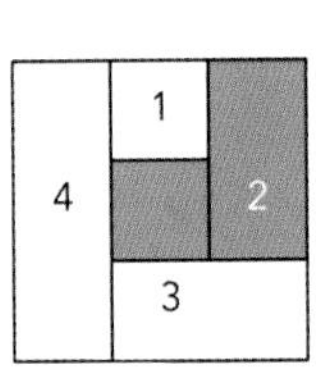

Round 1

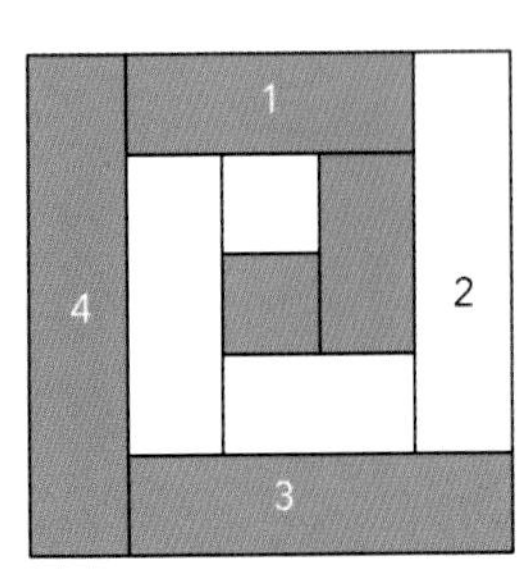

Round 2

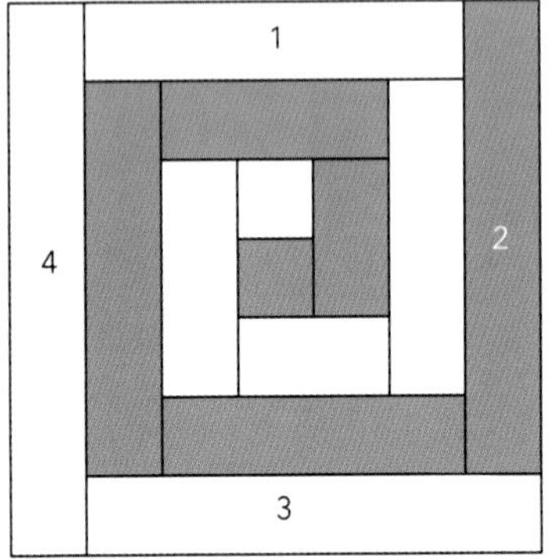

Round 3

QUARTER AND THREE-QUARTER LOG CABINS

Quarter and three-quarter log cabin blocks are less common than traditional four-sided ones but just as versatile, and can create great designs when multiple blocks are arranged together in a quilt top.

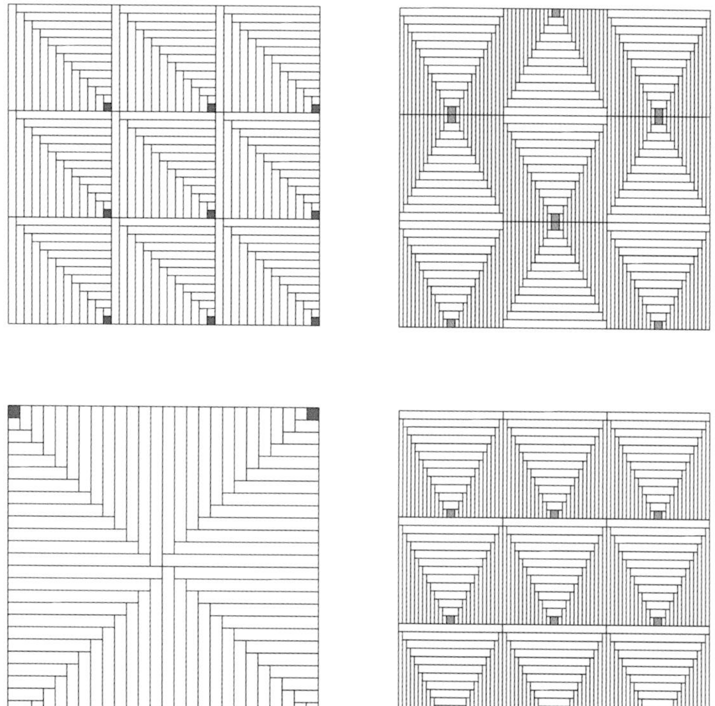

A few examples of multiple quarter and three-quarter block arrangements.

The fundamental technique for making quarter and three-quarter blocks is the same as for four-sided blocks, but instead of sewing logs on all four sides of the centre, you sew logs only on two sides for quarter log cabins and three sides for three-quarter log cabins.

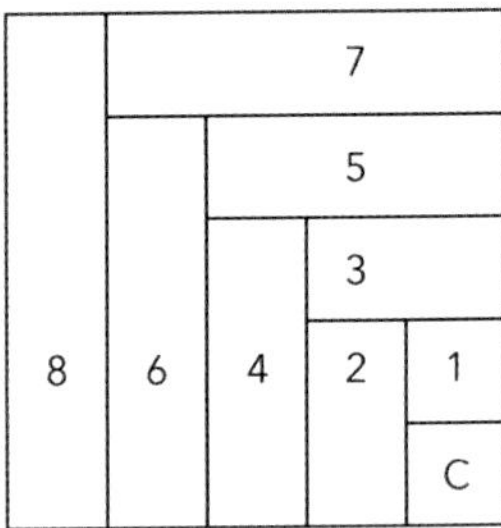

Quarter log cabin

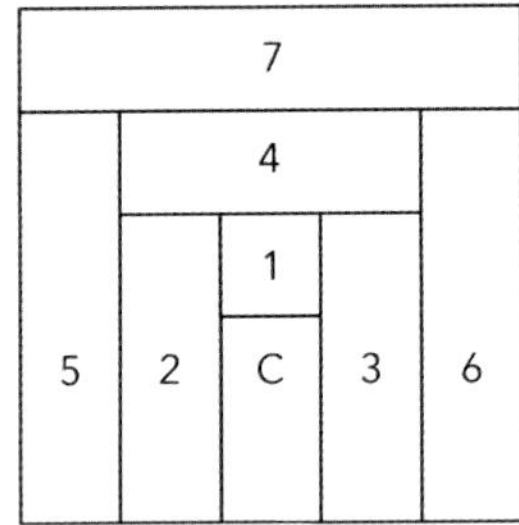

Three-quarter log cabin

It's more difficult to keep the sides straight when sewing logs on only two or three sides, especially if you cut your logs as you go. I find it's easier to make my block slightly bigger and trim it down to size once I've finished. To achieve this, cut your logs a bit longer than needed. It's better to trim down your block than come up short. (See Block 74, which has been left untrimmed.)

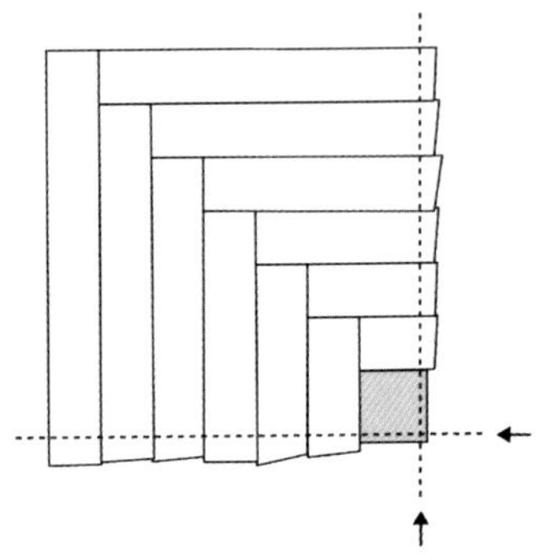

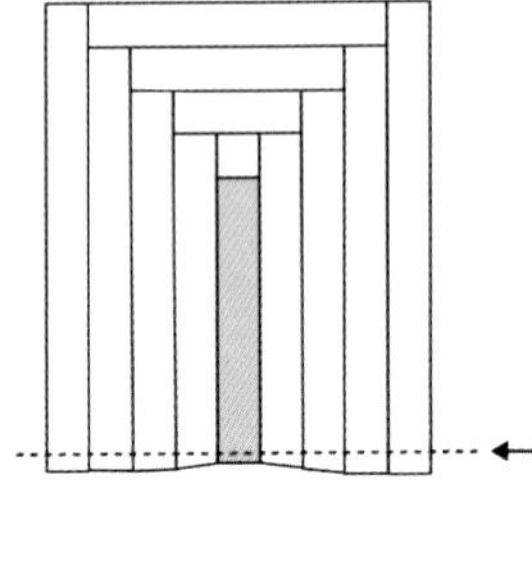

Leave a bit of length to your logs when you sew, and trim your block at the end.

CURVED BLOCKS

By playing with the width ratio of logs and using contrasting colours, you can create curves in your log cabin block. This in turn can create countless patterns when blocks are repeated. Some Japanese log cabin quilts are great examples.

There are three main ways to create a curve in a log cabin block:

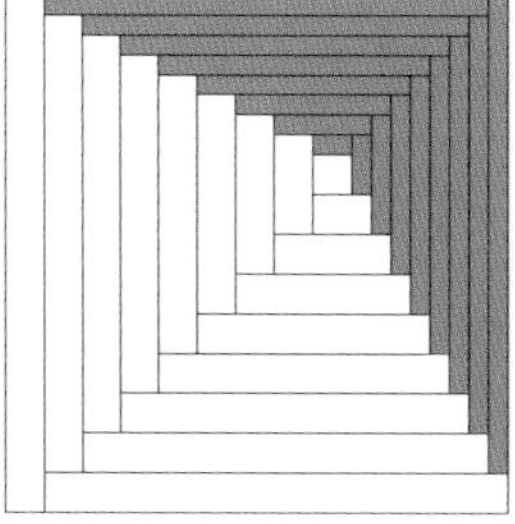

1:2 ratio

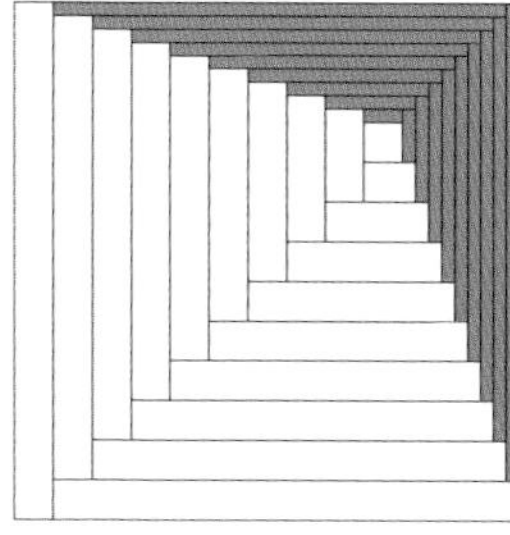

1:3 ratio

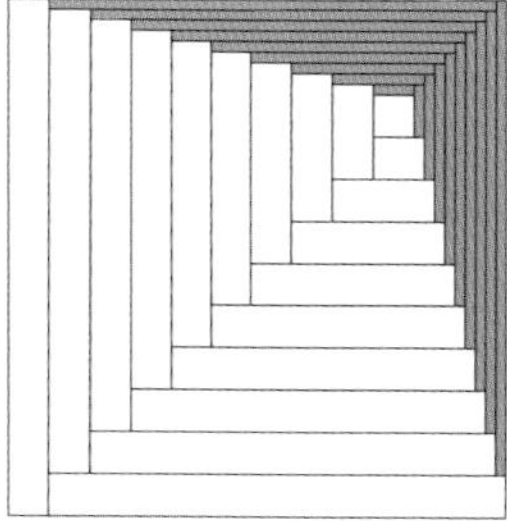

1:4 ratio

1. When the logs on two adjacent sides of a block are narrower than the logs on the opposite sides, it creates a slight curve in the design.
2. The second way to create curves is to increase/decrease the width of the logs with every round or every other round. Block 48 demonstrates this: on two adjacent sides the width increases by ½" (1.3cm) every two rounds; on the opposite two adjacent sides the width decreases by ¼" (0.6cm) every two rounds.

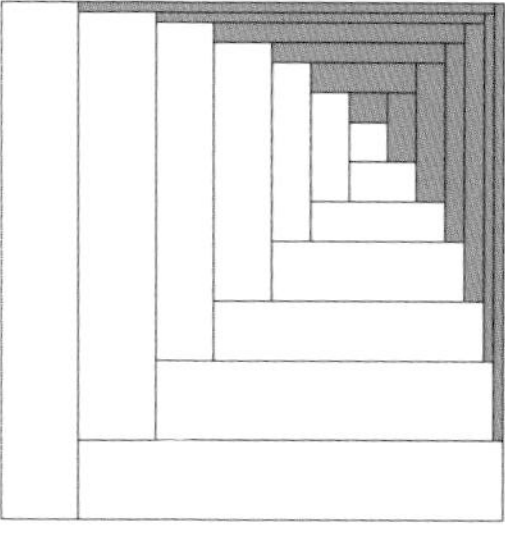

Increasing and decreasing widths.

3. The third way to create curve is to use two sets of strips with a width ratio of 1:2, and swap which one you use on a given side halfway. Block 49 is built like a courthouse steps log cabin, and for the first four rounds two opposite sides have ½" (1.3cm) logs and the other two opposite sides have 1" (2.5cm) logs. The width of logs is reversed for the next four rounds, creating a more pronounced curve. Multiple iterations of this block can create a design with full circles.

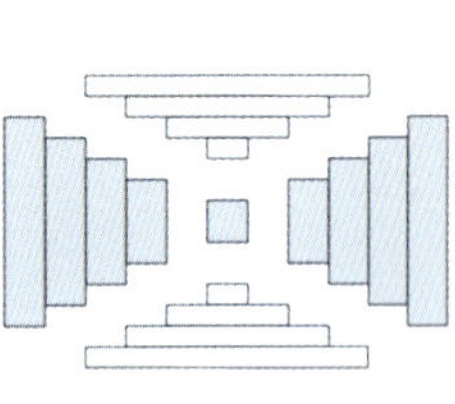

Rounds 1 to 4 of Block 49.

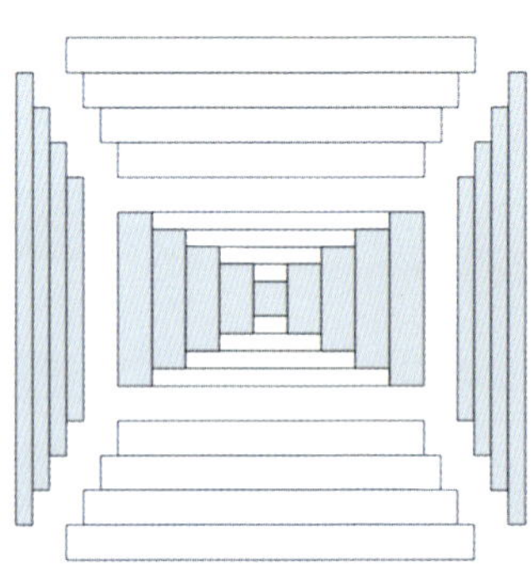

Rounds 5 to 8 of Block 49.

Variations on this technique yield very different outcomes: Block 50 is pieced clockwise and the narrow/wide strips are positioned on adjacent sides; Block 51 keeps the courthouse steps piecing direction but with the narrow/wide strips on adjacent rather than opposite sides like Block 49.

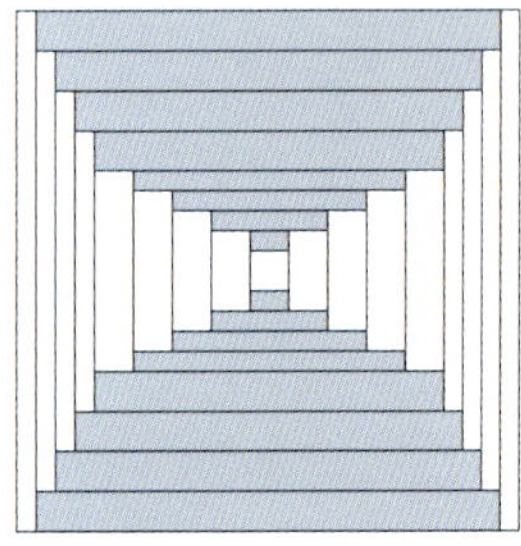

Block 49

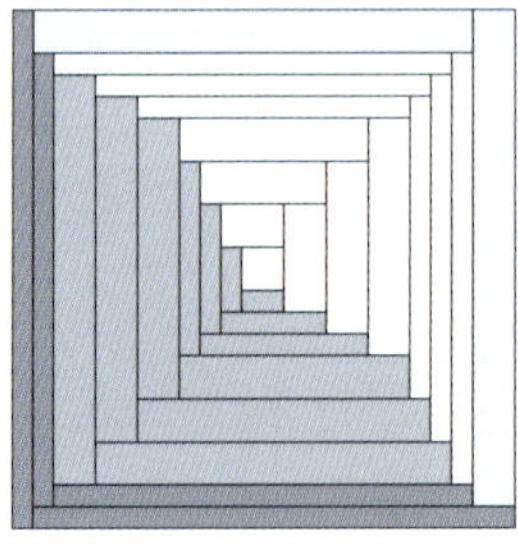

Block 50

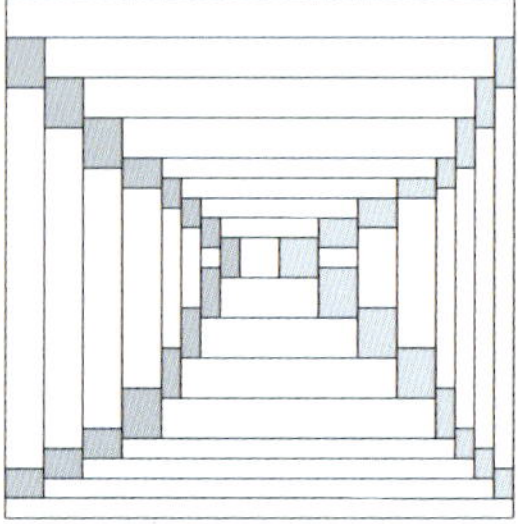

Block 51

POLYGON AND CRAZY LOG CABINS

The basic principle of the log cabin block can easily be applied to centres that are not square or rectangular: you go around the centre, adding logs one side at a time. You can find online examples of quilts made with triangular or hexagonal log cabin blocks, which are more common as these shapes can tessellate to form a quilt top.

POLYGON LOG CABIN

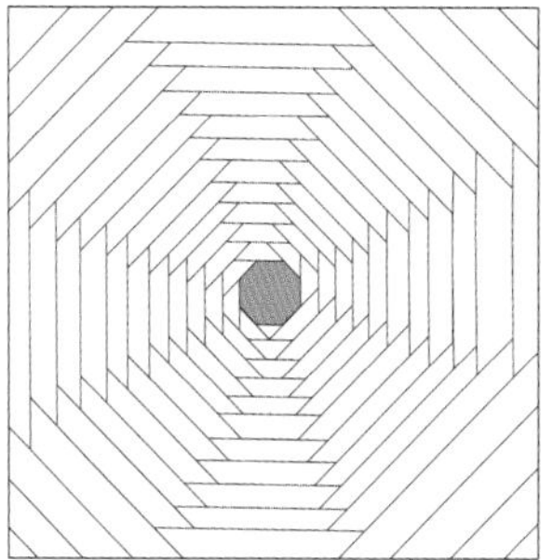

For this book I have used centres that have 3, 5, 6, 7 and 8 sides and created square blocks using the fabric foundation piecing technique. These are free form, improvised blocks. I have decided to make them square, but you can keep the polygonal shape and trim your foundation fabric around it.

A note on estimating the length of logs: your logs will need to be longer than the sides they are going to be stitched on, and how long they need to be will vary depending on how many sides your centre has (more specifically how wide the angles are at the corners), the length of the polygon's side, and how wide your logs are. I wish there was a formula for this but, short of having one, use scrap fabric or pieces of paper to give you an idea of what you're aiming for. It's roughly the length of the side of the polygon plus twice the width of the strips plus a bit more. The narrower the angles, the longer your strip needs to be. There's no downside to being overly generous (the extra is hidden under the next round of logs), but every downside to cutting them too short: you will have a visible raw edge. The first two rounds are the trickiest, then it gets easier as your sides get longer.

Also bear in mind that, if your centre is very off-centre, you will need to add more logs to certain sides to cover the surface of the foundation fabric (see Block 79). If your aim is to cover the whole surface of your foundation fabric to have a square or rectangular block, your logs will need to spill out at the edges and then be trimmed down, as the logs will come at an angle. See Blocks 76 and 80 for examples of untrimmed blocks.

To make a polygon log cabin block:

1. Start by cutting a piece of foundation fabric, 1" (2.5cm) wider in all directions than your desired finished size.
2. Cut your centre, either using a polygon template (easily found online or created using a drawing or word processing software) or cutting it freehand. Your centre needs to have seam allowance on all sides.
3. Position your centre on your foundation fabric and secure it with a pin or a dot of fabric glue. Your centre can be in the middle, or offset.
4. Prepare your logs by cutting strips of fabric. The more sides there are to your centre, the more fabric you will need.
5. Cut your first log (longer than needed, see previous page).
6. Stitch the first log onto the first side of your polygon using a ¼" (0.6cm) seam allowance. Your seam needs to go along the full length of the log. Flip the log outwards and iron it.
7. Cut the second log so that it overlaps with the first one. Stitch in place, flip then iron.
8. Carry on until you have added a full round. Start the second round on the same side of the polygon where the first log was sewn. Continue until you have covered the whole surface of your foundation fabric, then trim to desired size. Alternatively, you can leave your block as a polygon.

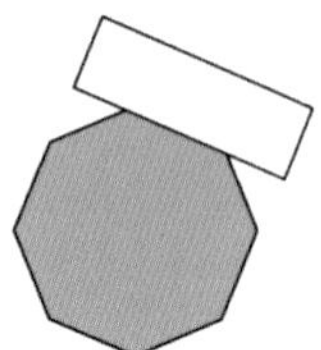
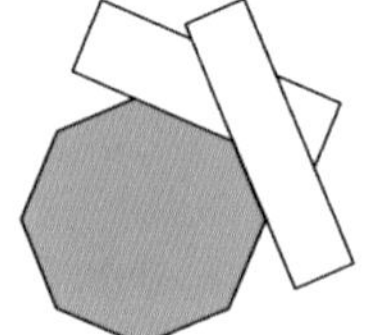
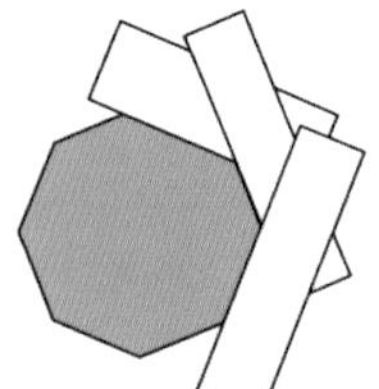

This is what your block will look like when you sew the first round on a polygonal centre.

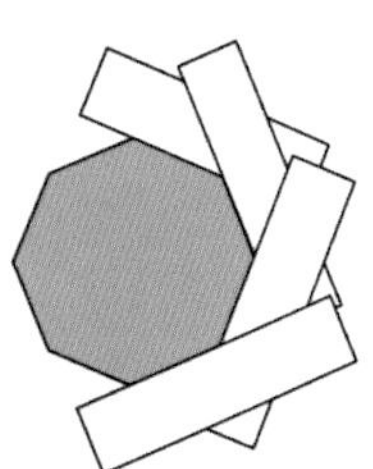
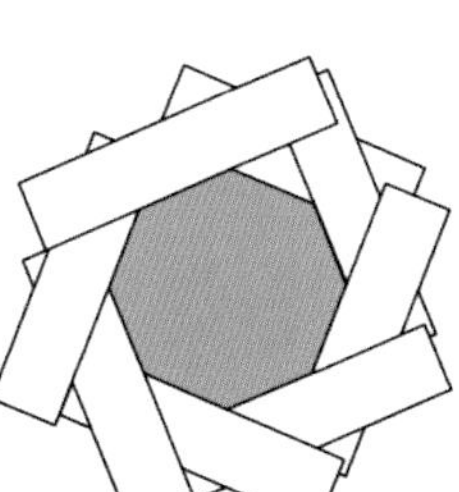
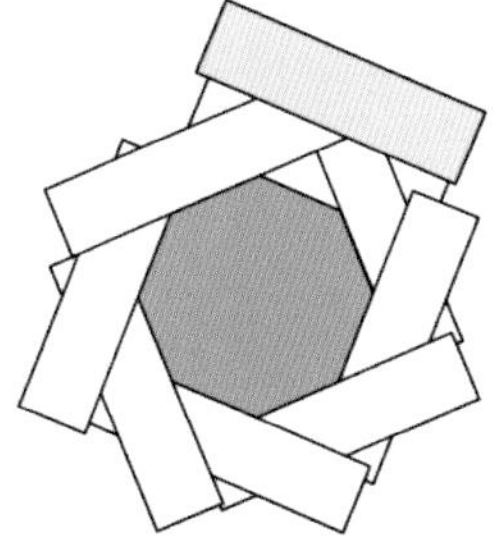

First log of the second round.

CRAZY LOG CABIN

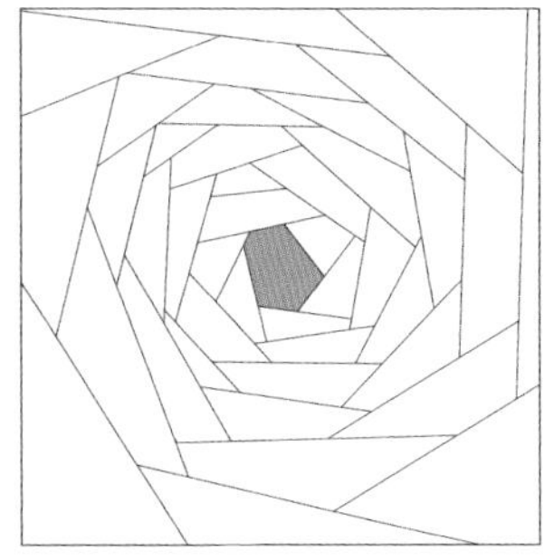

The crazy log cabin is a variation of the polygon block in which the width of the logs and their placement are less systematic. These blocks are improvised and no two blocks will look the same.

Despite the improvised nature of the block, it helps to do a bit of planning and try out various configurations before sewing the logs in place. Blocks 81 and 82 are made using the fabric foundation piecing method with fabric scraps and remnants.

Following the instructions for fabric foundation piecing on page 144:

1. Start with a generous centre, so you have a bit of flexibility when placing the logs. Gather the strips of fabric you intend to use as logs. You can use scraps of different widths and lengths.
2. Position your centre on your foundation fabric.
3. Arrange the strips around your centre, varying the angles and making sure that no (or very few) adjacent strips are parallel with each other. You do not have to cover the whole surface but it's a good idea to plan one or two rounds ahead of sewing.
4. When you are happy with your arrangement, take a photo to remind yourself of your pattern.
5. Remove the strips, then, following the photo you took, sew them around the centre in order, using the stitch and flip method, ironing each log outwards. For the double line crazy log cabin block (Block 82), I pieced thin strips of fabric scraps end to end, then sewed this long strip onto a wide strip of denim to create a double line strip.
6. Carry on until you have reached the desired size. Trim your block using a ruler and rotary cutter.

FULL CIRCLE AND FOUR BLOCKS VARIATIONS

As we have seen in the Architecture of the Log Cabin section, blocks can be repeated and stitched in a grid to create a pattern across the surface of the quilt.

If you put four curved blocks together you can get a full circle. Subtle effects can be obtained by altering the width ratio, using a centre that is the width of the narrow log rather than the wide log, adding more rounds of narrow logs than of wide logs (or vice versa) or by piecing two blocks clockwise and two anticlockwise and using two different colours for the wide logs, as in Blocks 86 and 90.

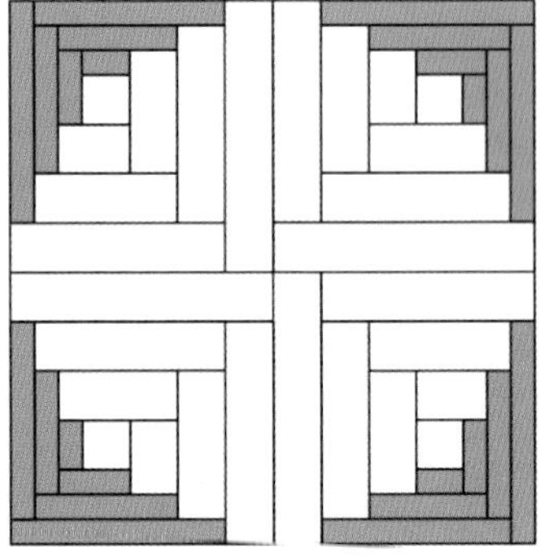

1:2 ratio with wide centre.

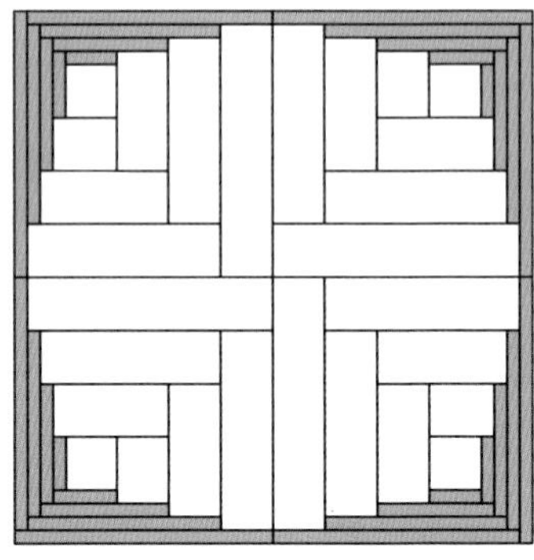

1:4 ratio with four rounds of wide logs and three rounds of narrow logs.

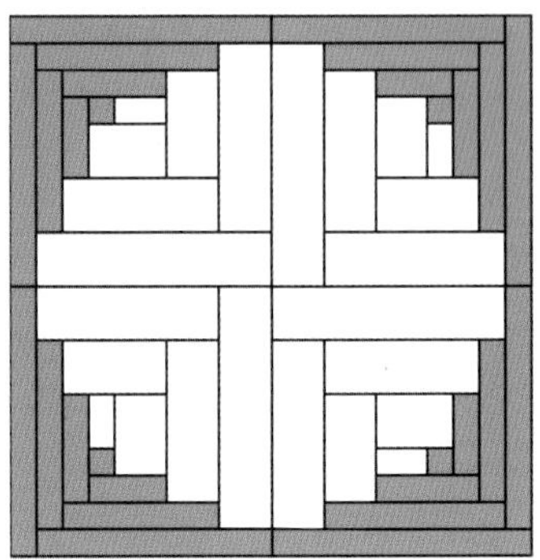

1:2 ratio with narrow centre.

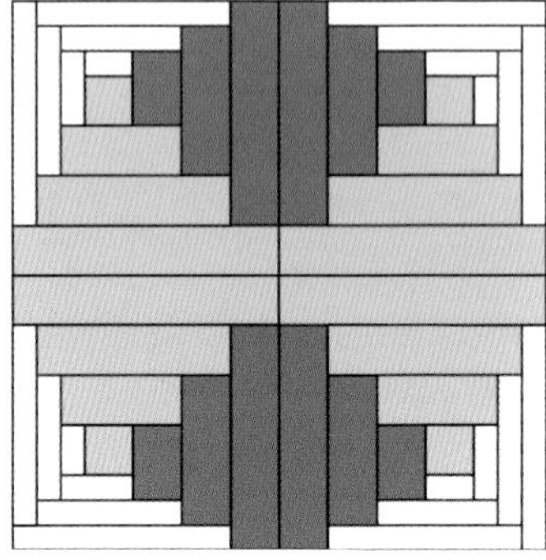

Mixing clockwise and anticlockwise blocks.

Beyond the full circle blocks, there are a lot of possibilities from simply repeating a block four times and sewing it in a 2 x 2 grid. Blocks 93 to 100 demonstrate that, and show that entirely new designs can be created by joining log cabins together. You can create your own, or like me take inspiration from traditional log cabin quilt patterns found in antique quilts.

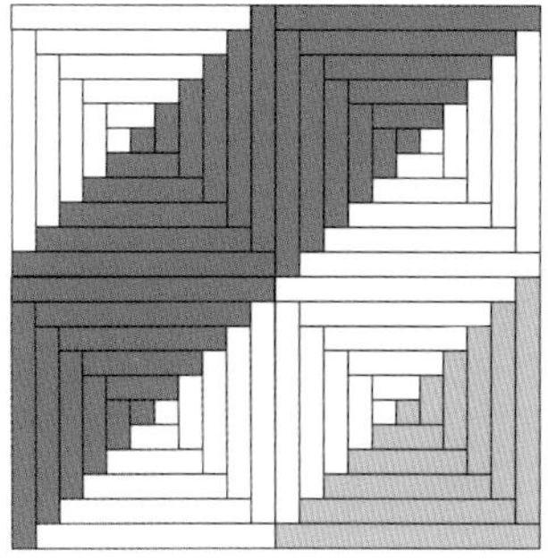

Fields and furrows design

Diamond log cabin design

Tips for sewing accurate blocks

As the blocks need to be of equal length and width to be sewn together, this is where some degree of accuracy is useful. Here are a few tips to achieve blocks of consistent size:

- Make sure the strips of fabric are of consistent width.
- Sew slowly and keep an eye on your seam allowance.
- If you are sewing without pins, make sure that your pieces are lined up properly and that the bottom fabric does not slip under the top one.
- Press the seam after each log is added.
- Trim your logs on a cutting mat with your ruler and rotary cutter instead of scissors.
- Square your four blocks down to the same size after each round of logs. Sometimes it's just a millimetre here and there, which can add up after a few rounds.

Sewing four blocks together

1. Arrange the blocks in a 2 x 2 grid.
2. Sew pairs of blocks together, press the seams.
3. Line up one pair of blocks on top of the other pair, making sure the central seams are lined up. Stitch the pairs of blocks together and press the seam.

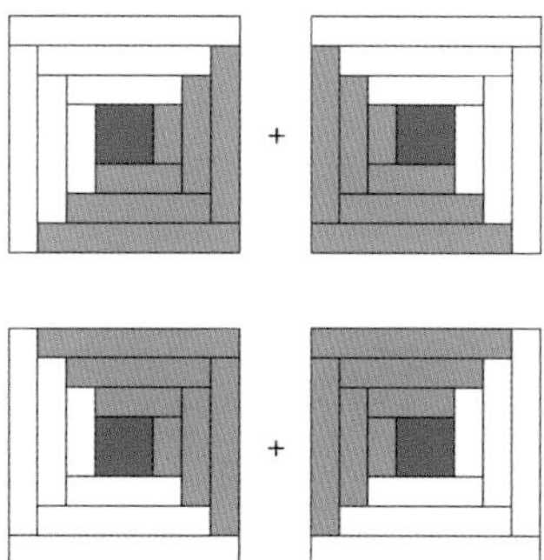

Join pairs of blocks first.

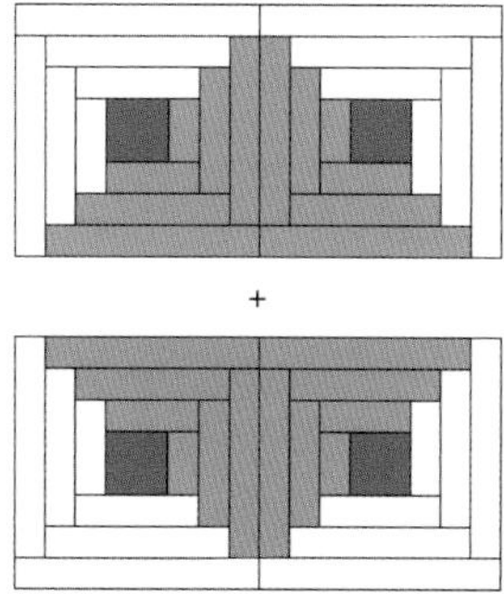

Then join the two halves.

Lining up seams

It can be tricky to line up two seams to get those perfect corners. Two methods can be used to make this easier. The first one consists of using the little ridge created by a sideways seam allowance to line up the central seam; the second is useful when lining up seams that have been ironed open.

Method 1: Nesting seams

1. Sew your two pairs of blocks together.
2. Press the seams sideways, with the seam on one pair of blocks pressed in one direction, and the seam of the other pair pressed in the opposite direction.
3. Line up the two pairs of blocks, right sides facing, using the little ridge from the seams to guide you and making sure they are as close as possible. This is called nesting the seams.
4. Use pins to keep the pieces from shifting. Stitch and press.

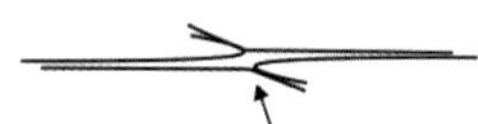

The little ridges from the seams will 'nest' neatly together.

Method 2: Using a pin and basting stitches:

1. Sew your two pairs of blocks together. Press your seams open.
2. Line up the two pairs of blocks, making sure the central seams are aligned. You can use a pin for this: go through the seam on the back of one block with a pin, then push it through the seam of the second block. Secure the pin by pushing it through the seams once more. Pin the rest in place.
3. Stitch your blocks together. Press.

If, like me, you sometimes find this a frustrating hit and miss process, consider basting the seam first, as basting stitches are easier to unpick:

1. Increase the stitch length on your sewing machine to the maximum and stitch your blocks together.
2. Remove the pins and check that the central seams are lined up and that you have neat corners. If the seams are not lined up: remove the basting stitches and start again. If the seams are lined up, set your stitch length back to normal and go over your basting stitches. There is usually no need to remove the basting stitches, unless they are visible from the front of your block.

FINISHING TOUCHES

SASHING

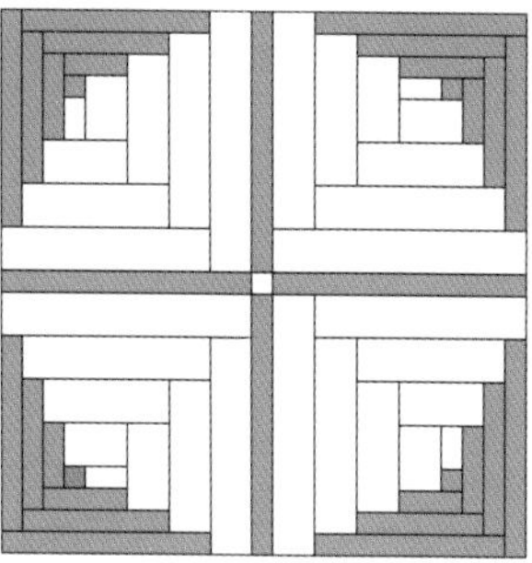

The strip of fabric separating individual blocks is called sashing, and it can be used creatively to add structure to a quilt. It can also usefully blur the lines when your individual blocks do not quite line up with each other.

To add sashing between blocks:

1. Cut a strip of fabric that is long enough to make a cross between your blocks (add a few inches to be on the safe side).
2. Join pairs of blocks with the sashing strip. Trim the strip flush with the edge. Press.
3. Join both pairs of blocks with the sashing strip, making sure that your seams are lined up. Use a basting stitch if needed.

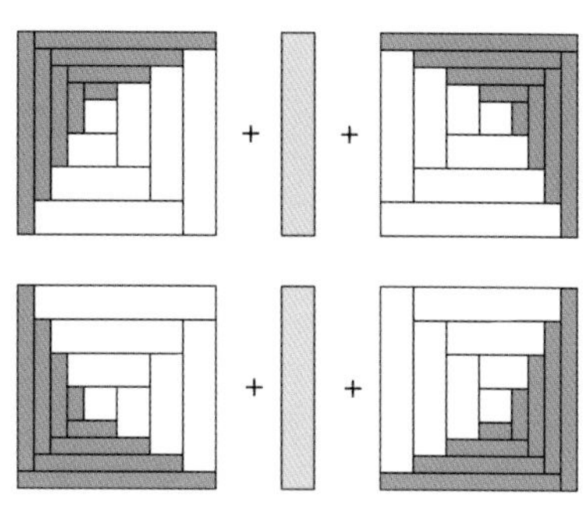

Join pairs of blocks with sashing.

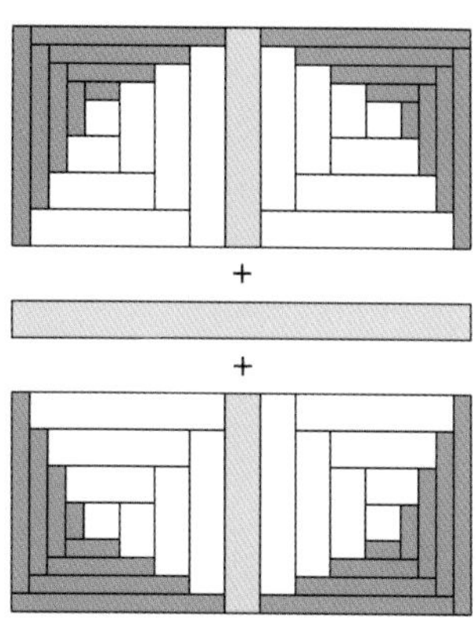

Join the two halves with sashing.

To add sashing with a central cornerstone:

1. Prepare your cornerstone: cut a square of fabric of the same length and width as your sashing + seam allowance.
2. Join pairs of blocks with the sashing strip. Trim the strip flush with the edge. Press.
3. Bookend your cornerstone with two strips of sashing and use this to join both pairs of blocks, making sure that the seams are lined up.

BORDER

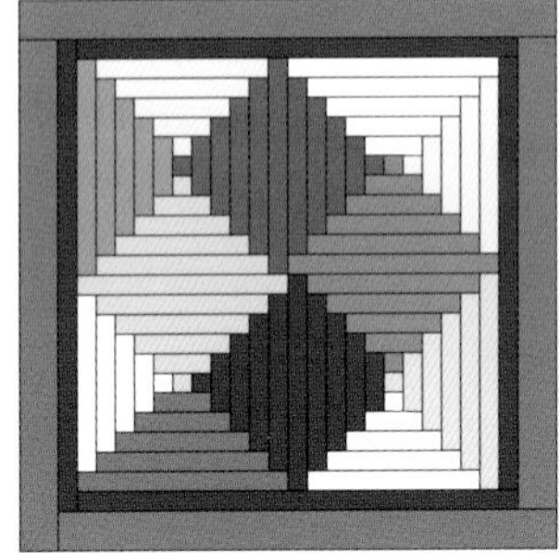

Adding a border is like framing an artwork: it will immediately make it look finished. It's also a good trick if you need a block to be bigger for a particular project.

The colour of the frame is very much up to you; it can match the outer layer of your block, match a colour within the block or contrast with it altogether. You can add a double border, a wide border, a border with cornerstones, etc. Adding a border is like adding one round of logs, just add a log on each side of your block.

BLOCK DIRECTORY

In this section, you will find a detailed description of each of the 100 blocks in the book. These patterns were my starting point, and will give you the measurements and the methods I have used.

The shading is used to highlight each block's structure and emphasize which part of the block should be made with contrasting fabric. Apart from the first 11 blocks, which differ only in piecing order and colour distribution, I have kept the shading to a minimum so you can treat the patterns as blank canvases and try out different things. If you would like to replicate the colour distribution of the original blocks, refer to the photographs in the first section of the book, pages 11–113.

A note on dimensions

When setting out to make the blocks for this book, I had to make a choice between making blocks that would all have matching finished sizes, or blocks that used a standard, easy to measure and scalable width of strips. I chose the latter, and the majority of the blocks in this book have been made with 1" (2.5cm) logs or increments of ¼" (0.6cm). When possible, I aimed to make blocks that came to 13" x 13" (33 x 33cm), but, because some blocks have a different size centre or use a variety of widths for the logs, some of the finished blocks in the book have different sizes.

Your block's exact final dimensions are also likely to vary depending on your seam allowance, how much you trim away at each round, whether you are consistent when cutting your strips, whether every seam was ironed as sewn, etc.

If you are not particularly worried about accuracy but do need your blocks to have a consistent finished size, increase the size of the smaller blocks by either finishing them with a round made of wider logs (I prefer to be overgenerous and trim down to size), by adding rounds of logs until you have reached the desired size or by adding a border.

Fabric requirements

The table opposite gives you an estimate of the length of strips you will need to cut to make a typical block of 13" x 13" (33 x 33cm), using fabric from standard 45" or 60" (115cm or 152cm) wide bolts. This is the total length, plus a ¼" (0.6cm) seam allowance, plus an extra 10 per cent to be on the safe side. If your strips are on the shorter side, i.e. if you are working from a small cut of fabric or a fat quarter rather than with a piece of fabric that goes selvedge to selvedge, you will need to increase the total length of strips slightly, as you will have more waste or will lose a few inches by sewing the strips end to end.

Estimated length of strips to cut for one 13" x 13" (33 x 33cm) block

Width of logs (number of rounds)	Total length of strips	45" (115cm) selvedge to selvedge		60" (152cm) selvedge to selvedge	
		Number of strips to cut	*Width of fabric needed*	*Number of strips to cut*	*Width of fabric needed*
½"/1.3cm (12 rounds)	400" (1016cm)	9	9" (22.9cm)	7	7" (17.8cm)
¾"/1.9cm (8 rounds)	265" (673cm)	6	7½" (19.1cm)	4.5	6¼" (15.9cm)
1"/2.5cm (6 rounds)	200" (508cm)	4.5	7½" (19.1cm)	3.5	6" (15.2cm)

HOW TO READ THE PATTERNS

Difficulty score

1. Easy, basic block, with strips all the same width and piecing that either goes round the centre or in a courthouse steps pattern.
2. Easy construction but requires a certain amount of focus to achieve the desired effect, either because of a slightly complex colour change, or strips that are of different widths. Blocks that use very narrow strips of fabric or that are made using the fabric foundation piecing method are also in this category.
3. Intermediate blocks, which demand focus, some planning and extra steps like cornerstones, double line strips and pre-pieced centres.
4. Challenging constructions where multiple steps are required, like blocks with cornerstones and different widths of strips that need to be switched halfway, or any block that requires greater precision or joining four separate blocks. Not so much difficult as time consuming. Set an afternoon aside. There are two blocks which I have marked as '4+' due to their complex structure.

Measurements

The measurements for each block are the dimensions of the centre and the logs before adding the seam allowances. This is to allow you to add your own preferred seam allowance, and to scale the measurements up or down easily.

In parentheses are the dimensions in centimetres, which are rounded to one decimal point. If you are working in centimetres, feel free to adjust the widths to more manageable numbers. As long as you respect the proportions (in particular in blocks that have different width logs) you will have comparable results.

The conversion table below gives you the width of strips of fabric to cut for a ¼" (0.6cm) seam allowance.

Measurements with seam allowances

Width of log in block	Cut strips (Width + ¼" seam allowance)	Width of log in cm (rounded)	Cut strips in cm (Width + 0.6cm seam allowance)
¼"	¾"	0.6cm	1.9cm
⅜"	⅞"	1cm	2.2cm
½"	1"	1.3cm	2.5cm
¾"	1¼"	1.9cm	3.2cm
1"	1½"	2.5cm	3.8cm
1¼"	1¾"	3.2cm	4.5cm
1½"	2"	3.8cm	5.1cm
1¾"	2¼"	4.5cm	5.7cm
2"	2½"	5.1cm	6.4cm

Cornerstones

This indicates whether the cornerstones were pre-cut, or made to overlap (see pages 151–154).

Piecing direction

I have added information on the order I used to piece the blocks in the book: clockwise and anticlockwise, courthouse steps, top-sides-bottom. Clockwise and anticlockwise are often interchangeable with each other, but courthouse steps and top-sides-bottom, which create a distinct structure, are not. Directions for blocks where the piecing order matters are marked by an asterisk (*).

Number of rounds

This is the number of rounds in the blocks I made. Every block can be scaled up or down, but bear in mind that some blocks might not end up square if you do so (when multiple widths of logs are involved).

Sashing and borders

This is the width of the sashing and borders as seen in the blocks. The outer round of a block with rings of colours is not considered a border, even if it is made of contrasting fabric.

Seams and technique

Most blocks in this book are made using the basic method with seams pressed open. When this is not the case it is specified.

Finished size

The size indicated is the size you should have once the block is finished, but does not include the final seam allowance (if you plan to leave the block as is, i.e. not sewn with anything else, then it will measure ½" (1.3cm) more in width and length). If you are working in centimetres, bear in mind that some millimetres will be lost or added through rounding the dimensions to the nearest decimal point.

Basic Block Variation (pages 142–145)

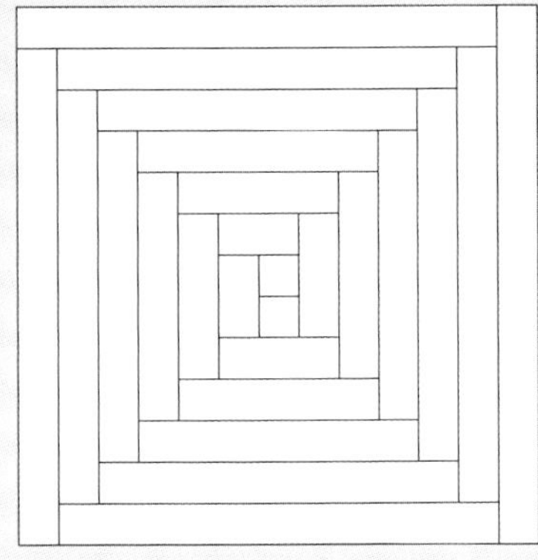

01

Difficulty: 1
Centre: 1" x 1" (2.5 x 2.5cm)
Logs: 1" (2.5cm)
Direction: clockwise
Rounds: 6
Finished size: 13" x 13" (33 x 33cm)

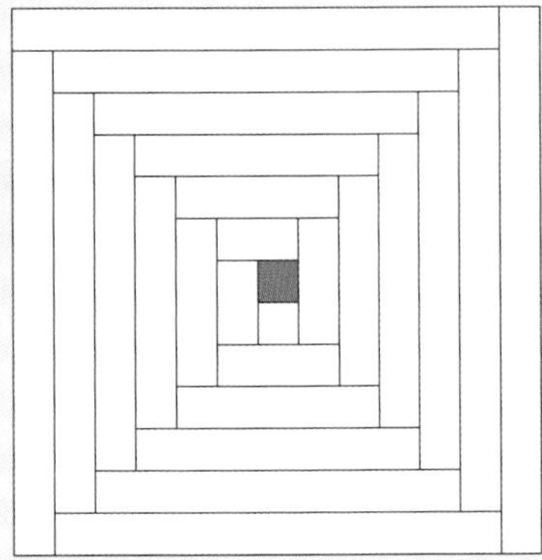

02

Difficulty: 1
Centre: 1" x 1" (2.5 x 2.5cm)
Logs: 1" (2.5cm)
Direction: clockwise
Rounds: 6
Finished size: 13" x 13" (33 x 33cm)

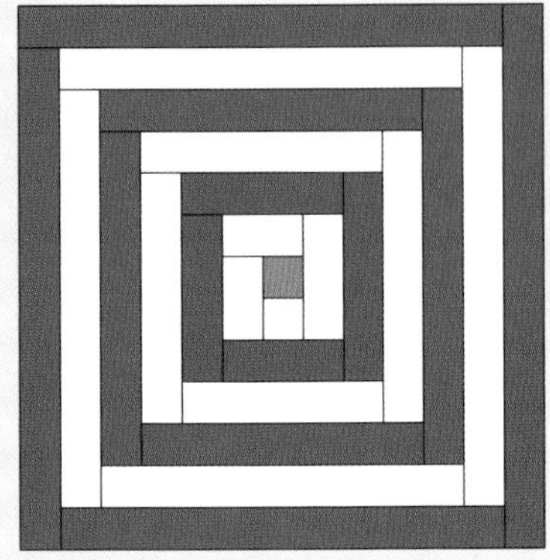

03

Difficulty: 1
Centre: 1" x 1" (2.5 x 2.5cm)
Logs: 1" (2.5cm)
Direction: clockwise
Rounds: 6
Finished size: 13" x 13" (33 x 33cm)

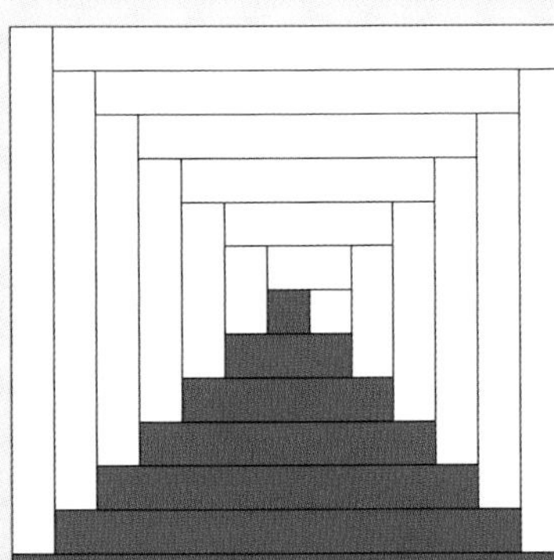

04

Difficulty: 1
Centre: 1" x 1" (2.5 x 2.5cm)
Logs: 1" (2.5cm)
Direction: anticlockwise
Rounds: 6
Finished size: 13" x 13" (33 x 33cm)

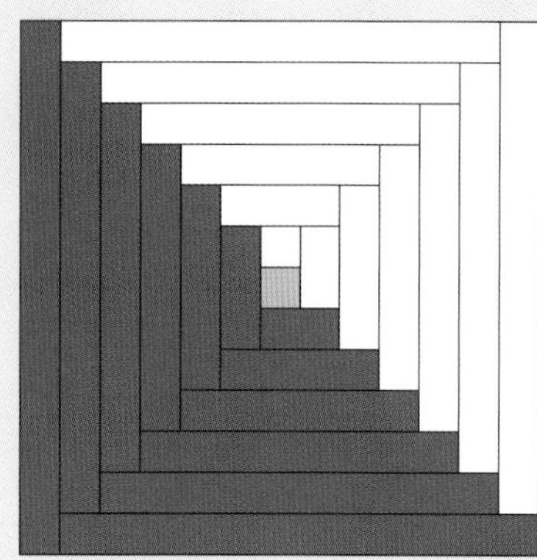

05

Difficulty: 1
Centre: 1" x 1" (2.5 x 2.5cm)
Logs: 1" (2.5cm)
Direction: clockwise
Rounds: 6
Finished size: 13" x 13" (33 x 33cm)

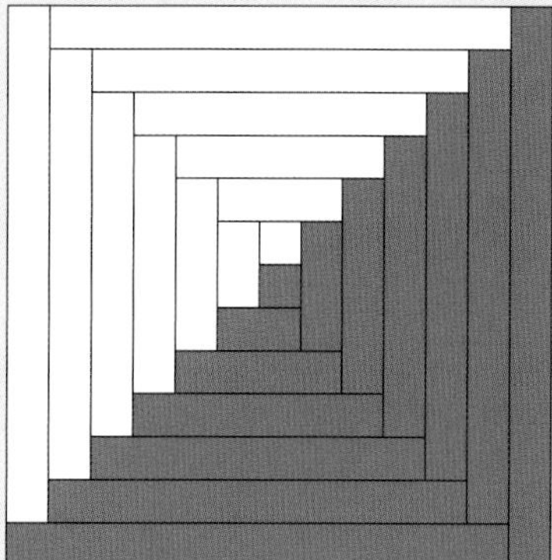

06

Difficulty: 1
Centre: 1" x 1" (2.5 x 2.5cm)
Logs: 1" (2.5cm)
Direction: anticlockwise
Rounds: 6
Finished size: 13" x 13" (33 x 33cm)

07

Difficulty: 1
Centre: 1" x 1" (2.5 x 2.5cm)
Logs: 1" (2.5cm)
Direction: *courthouse steps
Rounds: 6
Finished size: 13" x 13" (33 x 33cm)

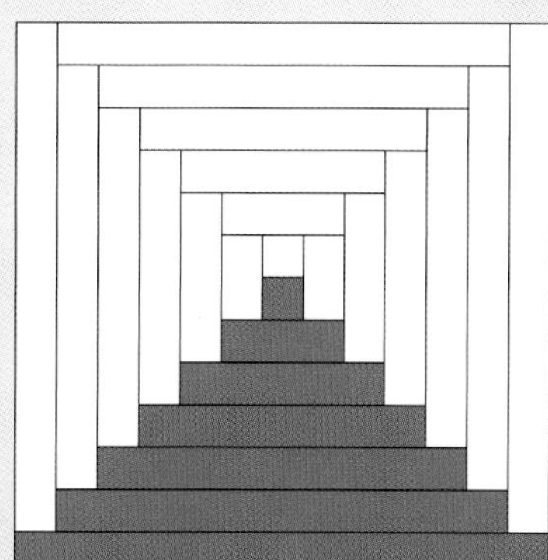

08

Difficulty: 1
Centre: 1" x 1" (2.5 x 2.5cm)
Logs: 1" (2.5cm)
Direction: *top-sides-bottom
Rounds: 6
Finished size: 13" x 13" (33 x 33cm)

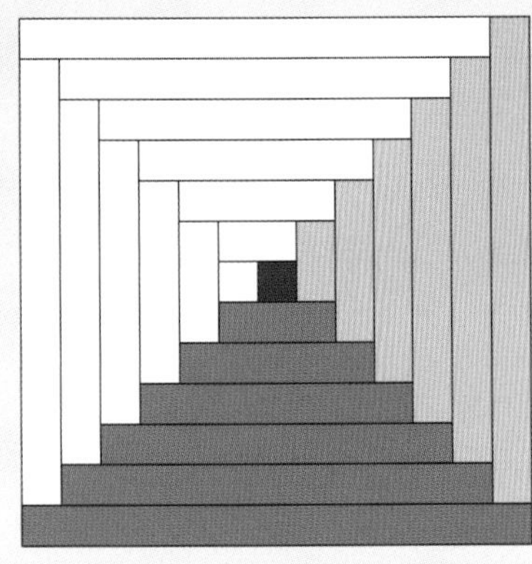

09

Difficulty:	1
Centre:	1" x 1" (2.5 x 2.5cm)
Logs:	1" (2.5cm)
Direction:	clockwise
Rounds:	6
Finished size:	13" x 13" (33 x 33cm)

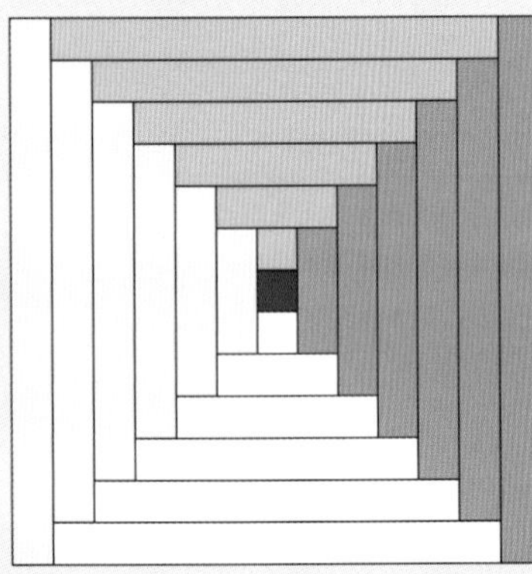

10

Difficulty:	1
Centre:	1" x 1" (2.5 x 2.5cm)
Logs:	1" (2.5cm)
Direction:	*courthouse steps
Rounds:	6
Finished size:	13" x 13" (33 x 33cm)

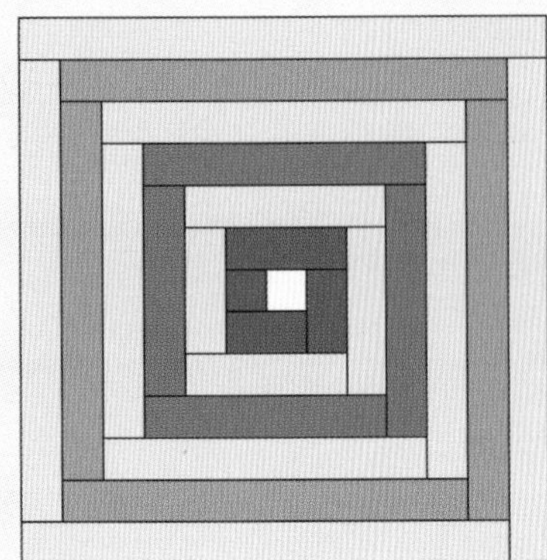

11

Difficulty:	1
Centre:	1" x 1" (2.5 x 2.5cm)
Logs:	1" (2.5cm)
Direction:	anticlockwise
Rounds:	6
Finished size:	13" x 13" (33 x 33cm)

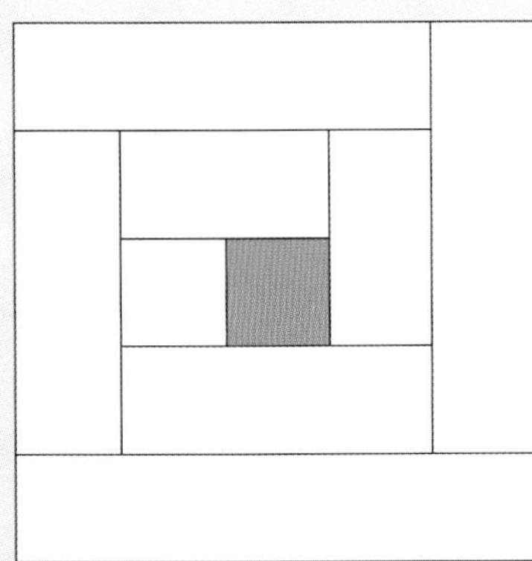

12

Difficulty:	1
Centre:	2½" x 2½" (6.4 x 6.4cm)
Logs:	2½" (6.4cm)
Direction:	clockwise
Rounds:	2
Finished size:	13" x 13" (33 x 33cm)

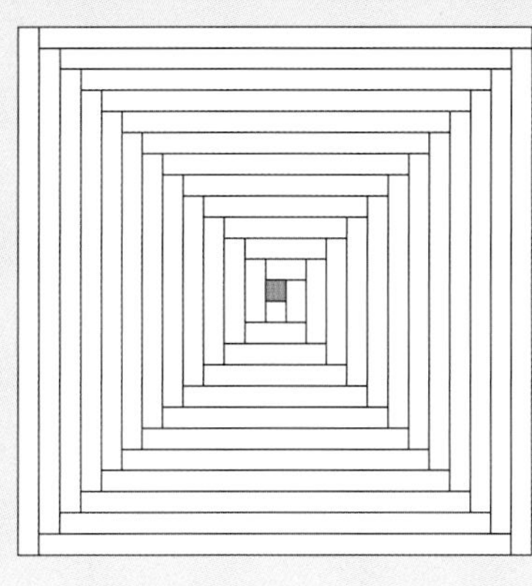

13

Difficulty:	2
Centre:	½" x ½" (1.3 x 1.3cm)
Logs:	½" (1.3cm)
Direction:	anticlockwise
Rounds:	12
Seams:	ironed inwards
Finished size:	13" x 13" (33 x 33cm)

Centre Variations (pages 146–149)

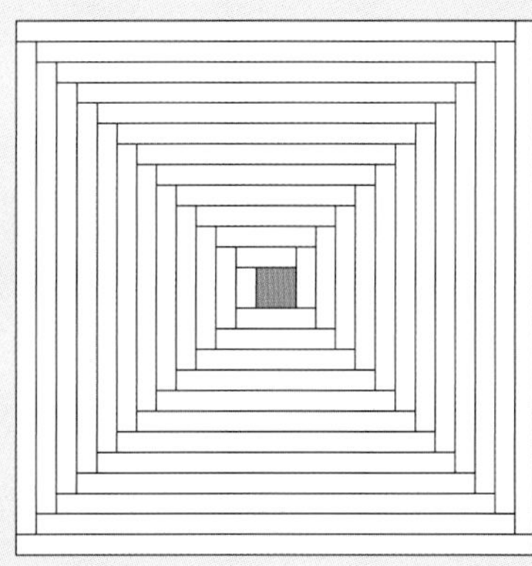

14

Difficulty:	2
Centre:	1" x 1" (2.5 x 2.5cm)
Logs:	½" (1.3cm)
Direction:	clockwise
Rounds:	12
Seams:	finger pressed
Finished size:	13" x 13" (33 x 33cm)

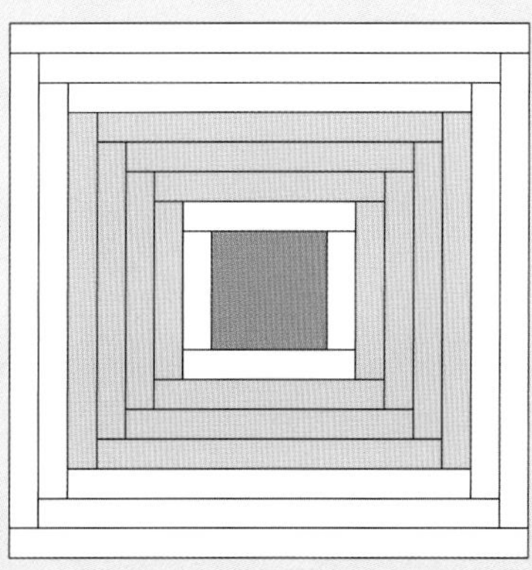

15

Difficulty:	2
Centre:	3" x 3" (7.6 x 7.6cm)
Logs:	¾" (1.9cm)
Direction:	*courthouse steps
Rounds:	7
Seams:	ironed outwards
Finished size:	13½" x 13½" (34.3 x 34.3cm)

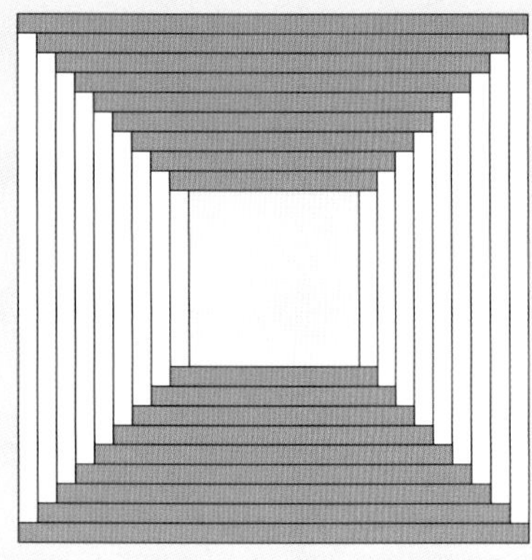

16

Difficulty: 2
Centre: 4½" x 4½" (11.4 x 11.4cm)
Logs: ½" (1.3cm)
Direction: *courthouse steps
Rounds: 9
Finished size: 14" x 14" (35.6 x 35.6cm)

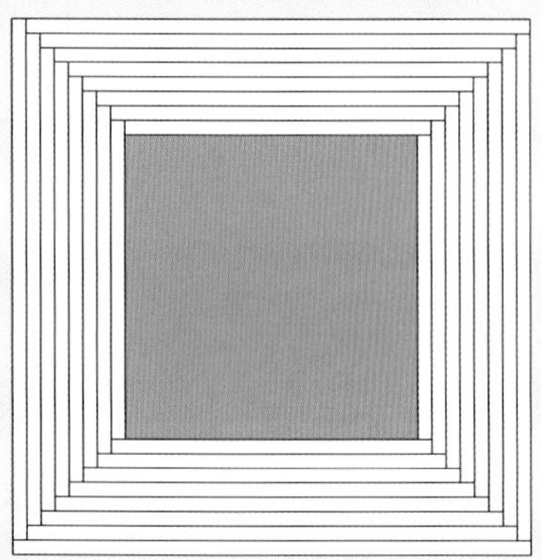

17

Difficulty: 2
Centre: 7" x 7" (17.8 x 17.8cm)
Logs: ⅜" (1cm)
Direction: anticlockwise
Rounds: 8
Seams: finger pressed
Finished size: 12½" x 12½" (31.8 x 31.8cm)

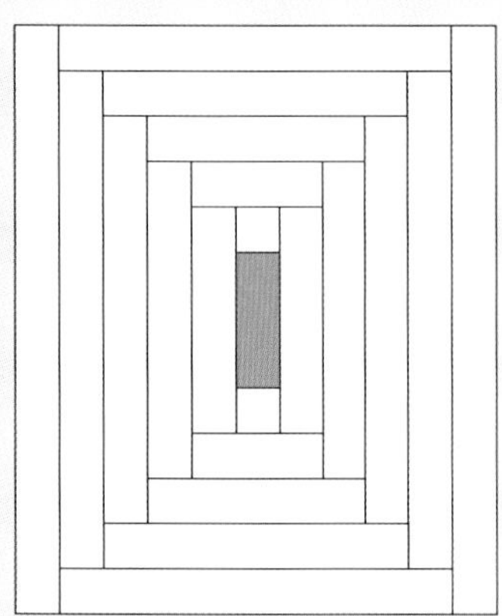

18

Difficulty: 1
Centre: 1" x 3" (2.5 x 7.6cm)
Logs: 1" (2.5cm)
Direction: *courthouse steps
Rounds: 5
Seams: ironed outwards
Finished size: 11" x 13" (28 x 33cm)

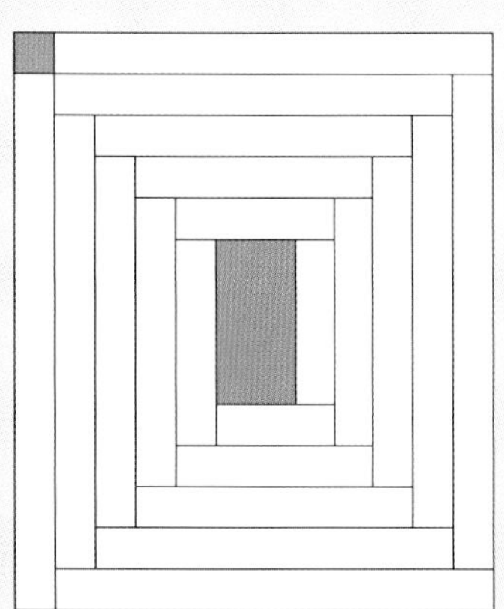

19

Difficulty: 2
Centre: 2" x 4" (5.1 x 10.2cm)
Logs: 1" (2.5cm)
Cornerstones: one 1" x 1" (2.5 x 2.5cm) on the last log
Direction: clockwise
Rounds: 5
Finished size: 12" x 14" (30.5 x 35.6cm)

20

Difficulty: 2
Centre: 2½" x 2½" (6.4 x 6.4cm)
(pieced with ½" (1.3cm) strips)
Logs: ¾" (1.9cm)
Direction: anticlockwise
Rounds: 7
Finished size: 13" x 13" (33 x 33cm)

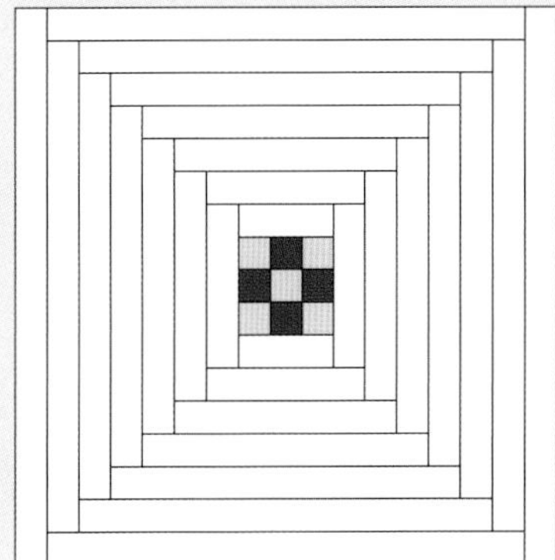

21

Difficulty: 2
Centre: 2¼" x 2¼" (5.7 x 5.7cm)
(pieced with ¾" x ¾" (1.9 x 1.9cm) squares)
Logs: ¾" (1.9cm)
Direction: *courthouse steps
Rounds: 7
Finished size: 13" x 13" (33 x 33cm)

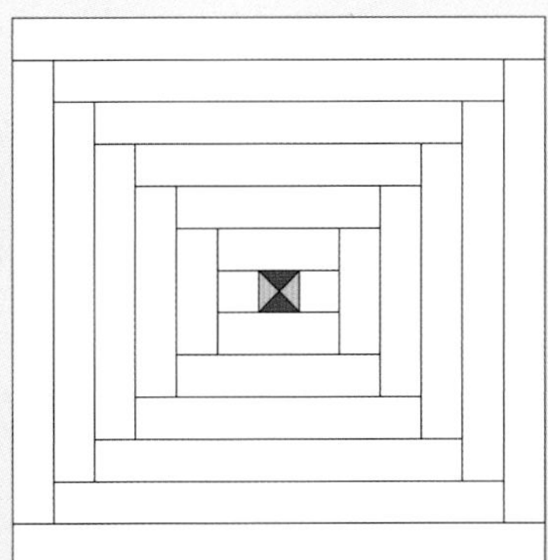

22

Difficulty: 2
Centre: 1" x 1" (2.5 x 2.5cm) (pieced)
Logs: 1" (2.5cm)
Direction: *courthouse steps
Rounds: 6
Finished size: 13" x 13" (33 x 33cm)

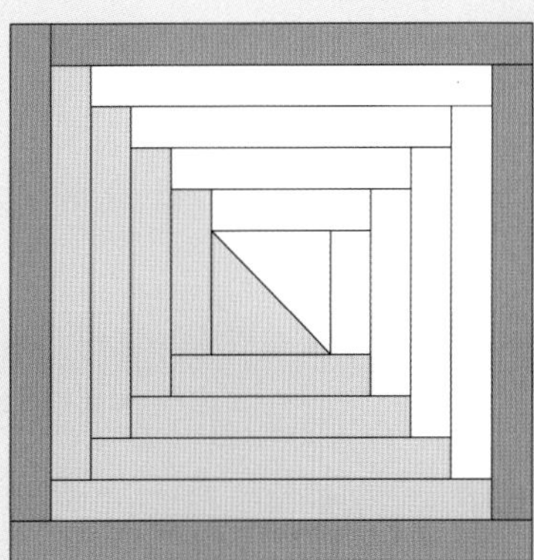

23

Difficulty: 2
Centre: 3" x 3" (7.6 x 7.6cm) (pieced)
Logs: 1" (2.5cm)
Direction: anticlockwise
Rounds: 4
Border: 1" (2.5cm)
Finished size: 13" x 13" (33 x 33cm)

Cornerstone Variations (pages 150–156)

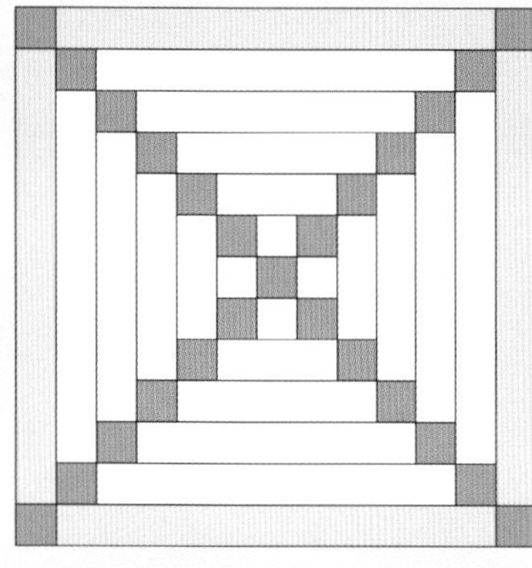

24

Difficulty: 3
Centre: 1" x 1" (2.5 x 2.5cm)
Logs: 1" (2.5cm)
Cornerstones: 1" x 1" (2.5 x 2.5cm)
Direction: clockwise
Rounds: 5
Border: 1" (2.5cm)
Finished size: 13" x 13" (33 x 33cm)

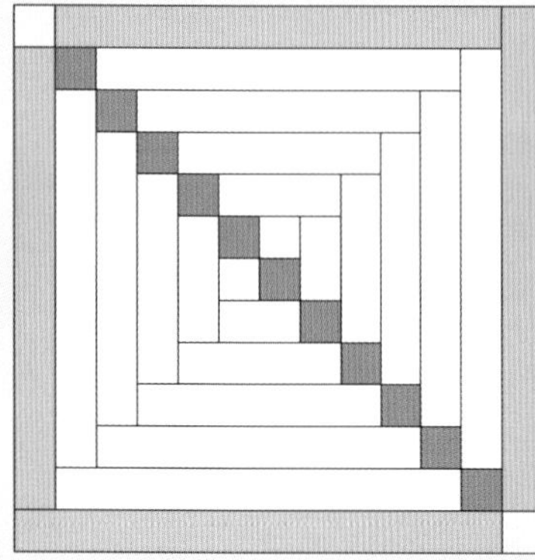

25

Difficulty: 3
Centre: 1" x 1" (2.5 x 2.5cm), same colour as cornerstones
Logs: 1" (2.5cm)
Cornerstones: 1" x 1" (2.5 x 2.5cm)
Direction: anticlockwise
Rounds: 5
Border: 1" (2.5cm)
Finished size: 13" x 13" (33 x 33cm)

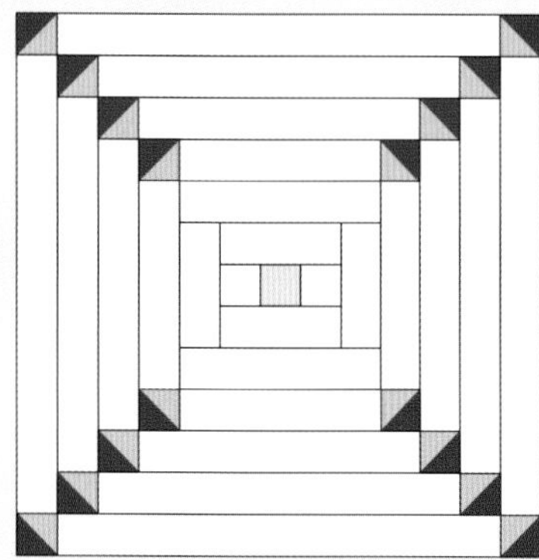

26

Difficulty: 4
Centre: 1" x 1" (2.5 x 2.5cm)
Logs: 1" (2.5cm)
Cornerstones: 1" x 1" (2.5 x 2.5cm) on rounds 3 to 6, with half square triangles
Direction: *courthouse steps
Rounds: 6
Finished size: 13" x 13" (33 x 33cm)

27

Difficulty: 4
Centre: 1" x 1" (2.5 x 2.5cm)
Logs: 1" (2.5cm)
Cornerstones: corner triangles on centre and 4 rounds
Direction: *courthouse steps
Rounds: 4
Border: 1½" (3.8cm)
Technique: fabric foundation piecing
Finished size: 14" x 14" (35.6 x 35.6cm)

Double Line and Stripe Effect Variations (pages 157–160)

28

Difficulty: 3
Centre: 1" x 1" (2.5 x 2.5cm)
Logs: 1" + ¼" (2.5 + 0.6cm) double line (narrow lines inwards)
Direction: *courthouse steps
Rounds: 6
Seams: narrow strip ironed towards wide strip
Finished size: 14½" x 14½" (36.8 x 36.8cm)

29

Difficulty: 3
Centre: 1" x 1" (2.5 x 2.5cm)
Logs: 1" + ¼" (2.5 + 0.6cm) double line (narrow lines outwards)
Direction: clockwise
Rounds: 6
Seams: narrow strip ironed towards wide strip in pre-pieced double line strips; seams between logs ironed open
Finished size: 14½" x 14½" (36.8 x 36.8cm)

30

Difficulty: 3
Centre: 1" x 1" (2.5 x 2.5cm)
Logs: ½" + ½" (1.3 + 1.3cm) double line for two sides & 1" (2.5cm) for two sides
Direction: anticlockwise
Rounds: 6
Finished size: 13" x 13" (33 x 33cm)

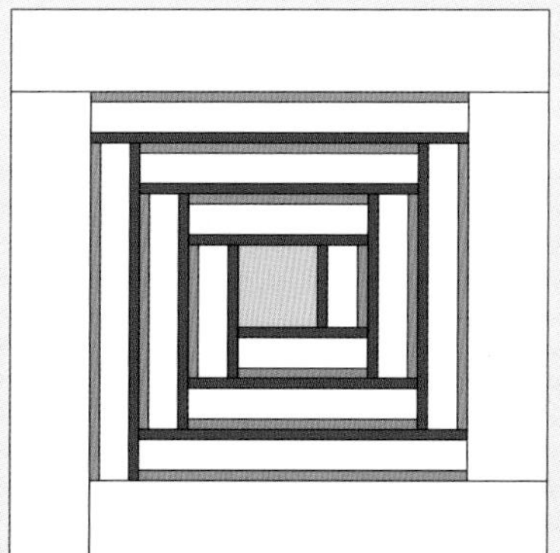

31

Difficulty: 3
Centre: 2" x 2" (5.1 x 5.1cm)
Logs: ¼" + ¾" + ¼" (0.6 + 1.9 + 0.6cm) triple line
Direction: clockwise
Rounds: 3
Border: 2" (5.1cm)
Seams: narrow strip ironed towards wide strip in pre-pieced triple line strips; seams between logs ironed open
Finished size: 14½" x 14½" (36.8 x 36.8cm)

32

Difficulty: 3
Centre: 1½" x 1½" (3.8 x 3.8cm)
Logs: 1½" (3.8cm) wonky double line
Direction: anticlockwise
Rounds: 3
Border: 1½" (3.8cm)
Finished size: 13" x 13" (33 x 33cm)

33

Difficulty: 3
Centre: 2" x 2" (5.1 x 5.1cm)
Logs: 1¼" + ⅛" (3.2 + 0.3cm) irregular (narrow lines outwards)
Direction: clockwise
Rounds: 4
Seams: narrow strips ironed towards wide strips
Finished size: 14" x 14" (35.6 x 35.6cm)

* Inspired by a block made by Jackie Davies in one of my workshops

34

Difficulty: 2
Centre: 2½" x 2½" (6.4 x 6.4cm)
Logs: 1" + 1" (2.5 + 2.5cm) double line
Direction: *courthouse steps
Rounds: 2
Border: 1" (2.5cm)
Finished size: 12½" x 12½" (31.8 x 31.8cm)

35

Difficulty: 2
Centre: 1" x 1" (2.5 x 2.5cm)
Logs: 1" (2.5cm)
Direction: clockwise
Rounds: 6
Finished size: 13" x 13" (33 x 33cm)

* Block traditionally known as 'Greek key' log cabin

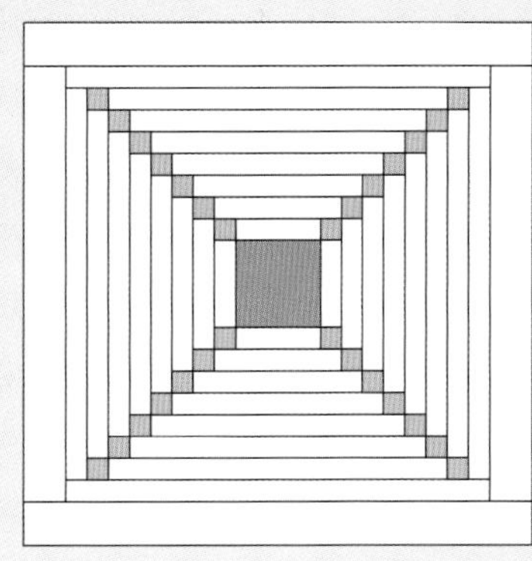

36

Difficulty: 4
Centre: 2" x 2" (5.1 x 5.1cm)
Logs: ½" (1.3cm)
Cornerstones: ½" x ½" (1.3 x 1.3cm) on rounds 1 to 7
Direction: courthouse steps
Rounds: 8
Border: 1" (2.5cm)
Finished size: 12" x 12" (30.5 x 30.5cm)

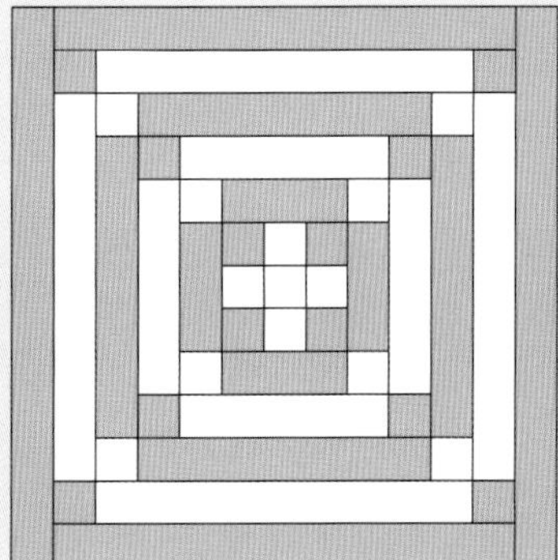

37

Difficulty: 3
Centre: 1" x 1" (2.5 x 2.5cm)
Logs: 1" (2.5cm)
Cornerstones: 1" x 1" (2.5 x 2.5cm) on rounds 1 to 5
Direction: courthouse steps
Rounds: 6
Finished size: 13" x 13" (33 x 33cm)

Two Widths Variations (pages 142–145)

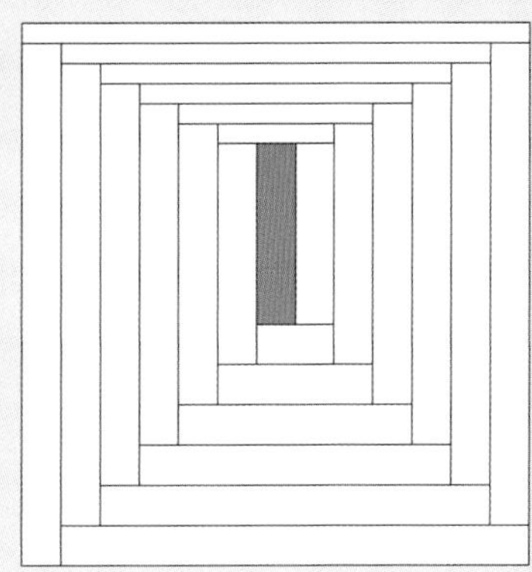

38

Difficulty: 2
Centre: 1" x 4" (2.5 x 10.2cm)
Logs: 1" (2.5cm) for 3 sides & ½" (1.3cm) for 1 side
Direction: clockwise
Rounds: 6
Finished size: 13" x 13" (33 x 33cm)

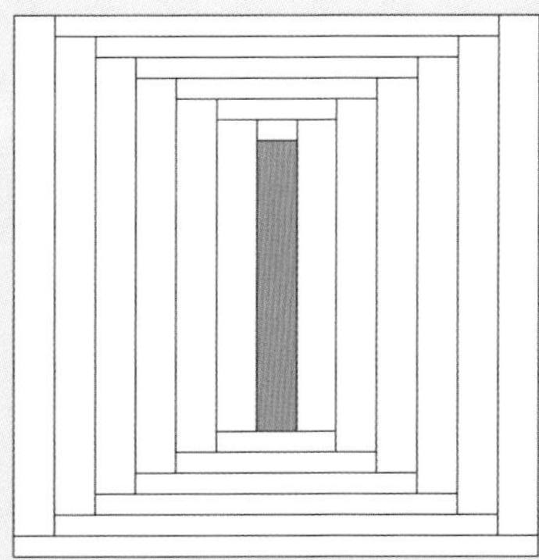

39

Difficulty: 2
Centre: 1" x 7" (2.5 x 17.8cm)
Logs: 1" (2.5cm) for 2 sides & ½" (1.3cm) for 2 sides
Direction: *top-sides-bottom
Rounds: 6
Finished size: 13" x 13" (33 x 33 cm)

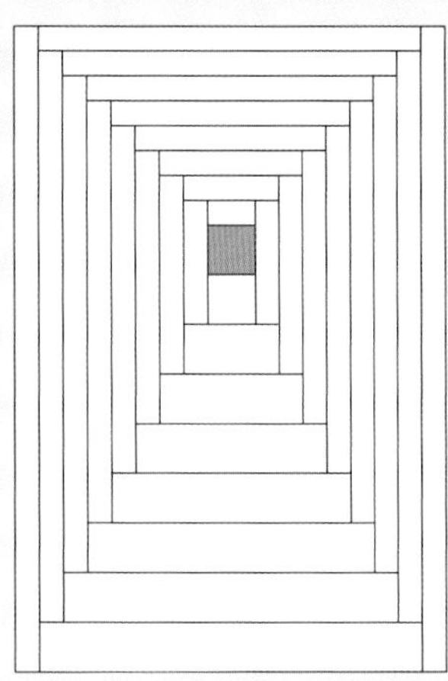

40

Difficulty:	2
Centre:	1" x 1" (2.5 x 2.5cm)
Logs:	1" (2.5cm) for 1 side & ½" (1.3cm) for 3 sides
Direction:	*courthouse steps
Rounds:	8
Seams:	ironed outwards on two sides
Finished size:	9" x 13" (22.9 x 33cm)

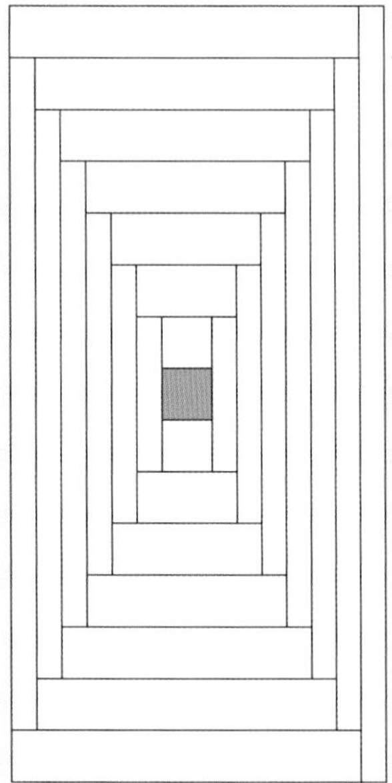

41

Difficulty:	2
Centre:	1" x 1" (2.5 x 2.5cm)
Logs:	1" (2.5cm) for 2 opposite sides & ½" (1.3cm) for 2 opposite sides
Direction:	*courthouse steps
Rounds:	7 (yellow side has only 6 logs in example)
Finished size:	7½" x 15" (19.1 x 38.1cm)

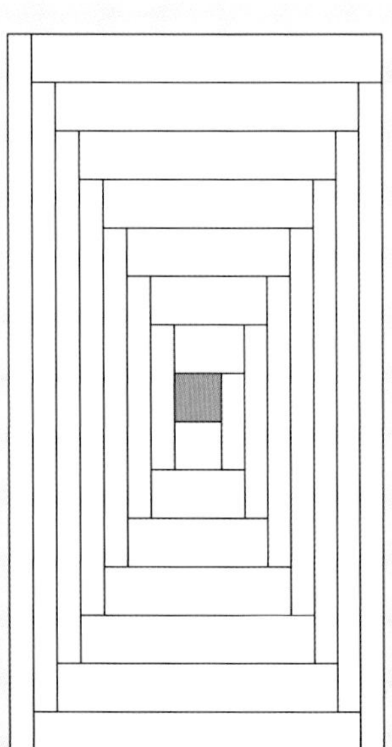

42

Difficulty:	2
Centre:	1" x 1" (2.5 x 2.5cm)
Logs:	1" (2.5cm) for 2 opposite sides & ½" (1.3cm) for 2 opposite sides
Direction:	anticlockwise
Rounds:	7
Finished size:	8" x 15" (20.3 x 38.1cm)

Curve Variations (pages 163–164)

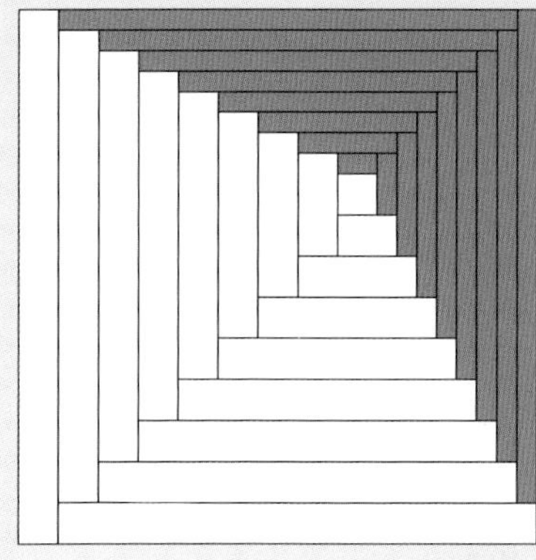

43

Difficulty:	2
Centre:	1" x 1" (2.5 x 2.5cm)
Logs:	½" (1.3cm) for 2 sides & 1" (2.5cm) for 2 sides
Direction:	clockwise
Rounds:	8
Finished size:	13" x 13" (33 x 33cm)

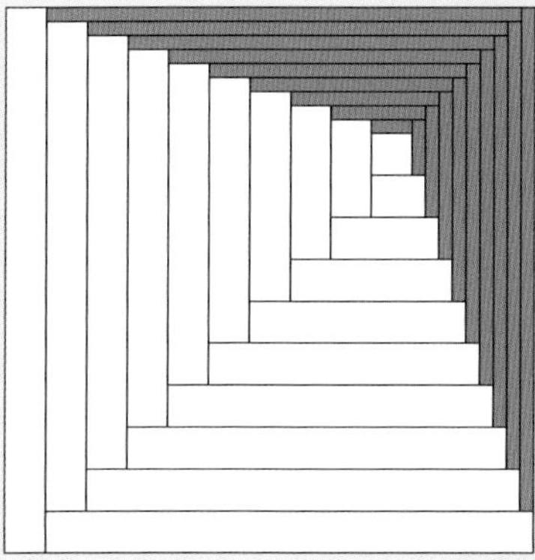

44

Difficulty:	2
Centre:	1" x 1" (2.5 x 2.5cm)
Logs:	⅜" (1cm) for 2 sides & 1" (2.5cm) for 2 sides
Direction:	clockwise
Rounds:	9
Seams:	narrow logs ironed outwards
Finished size:	13" x 13" (33 x 33cm)

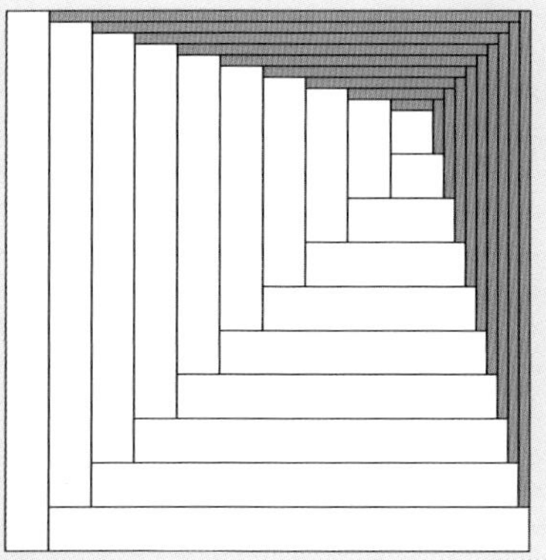

45

Difficulty:	2
Centre:	1" x 1" (2.5 x 2.5cm)
Logs:	¼" (0.6cm) for 2 sides & 1" (2.5cm) for 2 sides
Direction:	clockwise
Rounds:	9
Seams:	ironed outwards
Finished size:	12½" x 12½" (31.8 x 31.8cm)

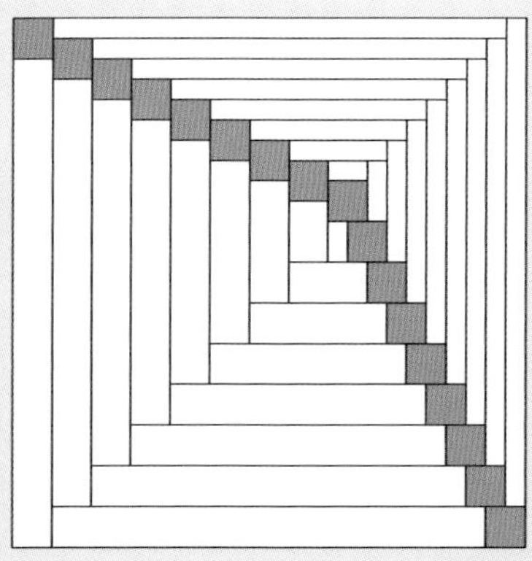

46

Difficulty:	3
Centre:	1" x 1" (2.5 x 2.5cm) (same colour as cornerstones)
Logs:	½" (1.3cm) for 2 sides & 1" (2.5cm) for 2 sides
Cornerstones:	1" x 1" (2.5 x 2.5cm) on wide logs
Direction:	clockwise
Rounds:	8
Finished size:	13" x 13" (33 x 33cm)

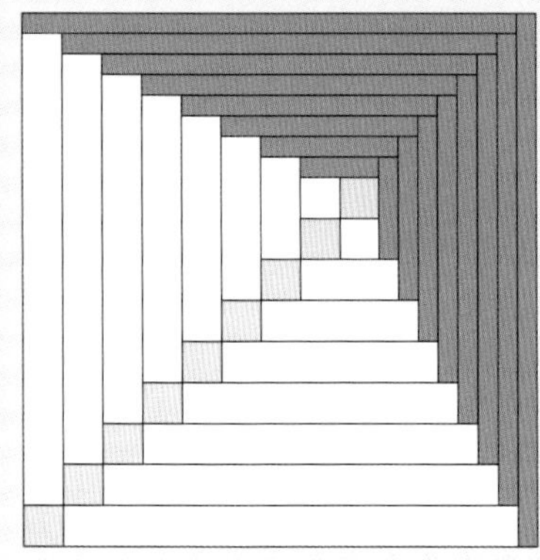

47

Difficulty: 3
Centre: 1" x 1" (2.5 x 2.5cm) (same colour as cornerstones)
Logs: 1" (2.5cm) for 2 sides & ½" (1.3cm) for 2 sides
Cornerstones: 1" x 1" (2.5 x 2.5cm) on wide logs (one side only)
Direction: clockwise
Rounds: 8
Finished size: 13" x 13" (33 x 33cm)

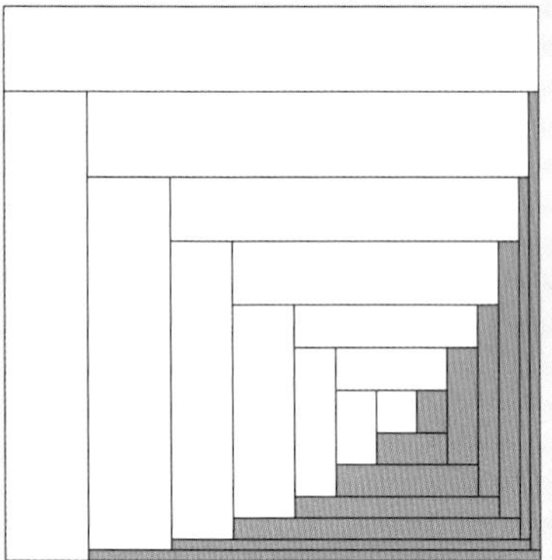

48

Difficulty: 4
Centre: 1" x 1" (2.5 x 2.5cm)
Narrow logs: (from centre outwards) ¾"; ¾"; ½"; ½"; ¼"; ¼" (1.9; 1.9; 1.3; 1.3; 0.6; 0.6cm)
Wide logs: (from centre outwards) 1"; 1"; 1½"; 1½"; 2"; 2" (2.5; 2.5; 3.8; 3.8; 5.1; 5.1cm)
Direction: clockwise
Rounds: 6
Finished size: 13" x 13" (33 x 33cm)

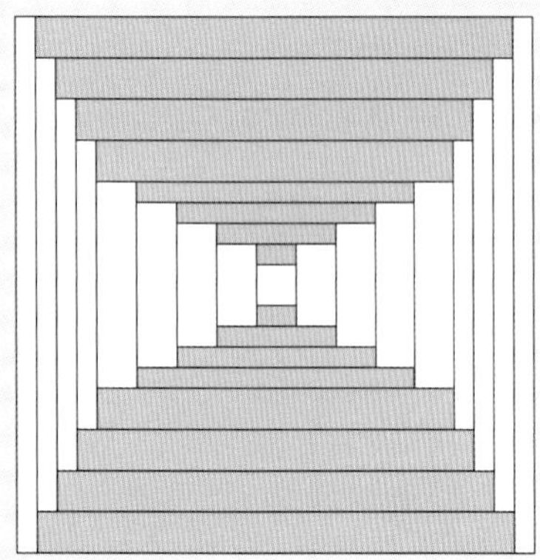

49

Difficulty: 4
Centre: 1" x 1" (2.5 x 2.5cm)
Logs: ½" (1.3cm) for 4 rounds then 1" (2.5cm) for 4 rounds (on opposite sides) & 1" (2.5cm) for 4 rounds, then ½" (1.3cm) for 4 rounds (on opposite sides)
Direction: *courthouse steps
Rounds: 8
Finished size: 13" x 13" (33 x 33cm)

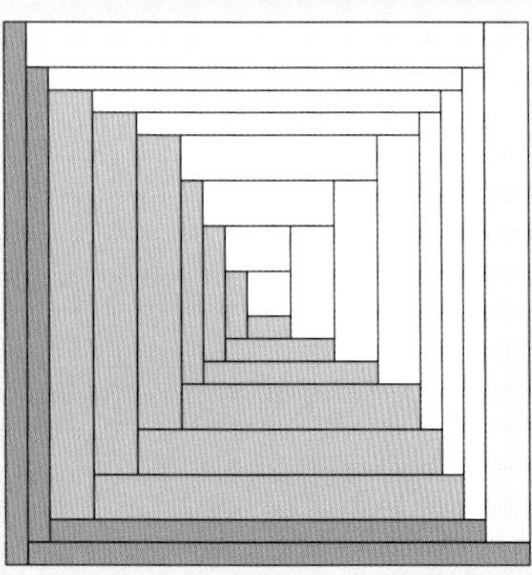

50

Difficulty: 4
Centre: 1" x 1" (2.5 x 2.5cm)
Logs: ½" (1.3cm) for 3 rounds then 1" (2.5cm) for 3 rounds on 2 adjacent sides & 1" (2.5cm) for 3 rounds then ½" (1.3cm) for 3 rounds on 2 adjacent sides
Direction: clockwise
Rounds: 6
Border: ½" (1.3cm) x 2 on 2 adjacent sides; 1" (2.5cm) on 2 adjacent sides
Finished size: 13" x 13" (33 x 33cm)

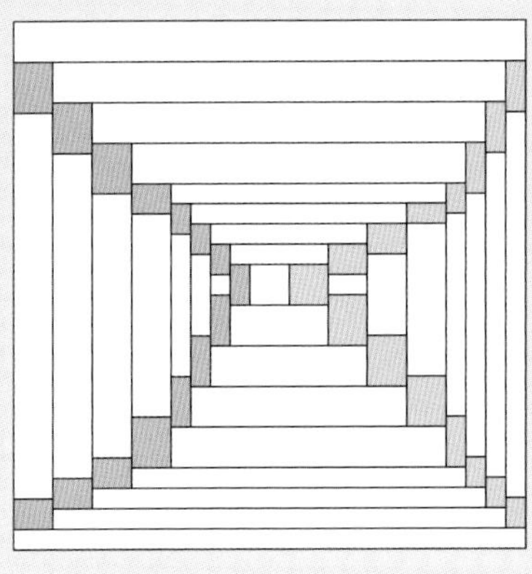

51

Difficulty:	4+
Centre:	1" x 1" (2.5 x 2.5cm)
Logs:	1" (2.5cm) for 4 rounds then ½" (1.3cm) for 4 rounds (2 adjacent sides) & ½" (1.3cm) for 4 rounds then 1" (2.5cm) for 4 rounds (2 adjacent sides)
Cornerstones:	on opposite sides (overlapping)
Direction:	*courthouse steps
Rounds:	8
Finished size:	13" x 13" (33 x 33cm)

Three Widths Variations (pages 142–145)

Width of logs listed from first log to fourth, in the order they are sewn around the centre.

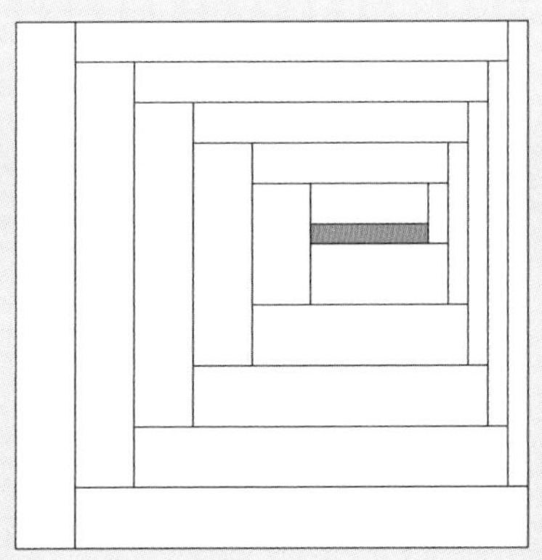

52

Difficulty:	2
Centre:	3" x ½" (7.6 x 1.3cm)
Logs:	1"; ½"; 1½"; 1½" (2.5; 1.3; 3.8; 3.8cm)
Direction:	clockwise
Rounds:	5
Finished size:	14" x 14" (35.6 x 35.6cm)

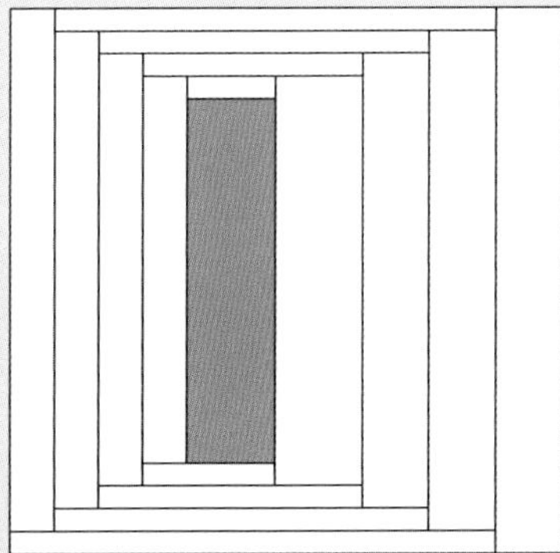

53

Difficulty:	2
Centre:	2" x 8" (5.1 x 20.3cm)
Logs:	½"; 1"; ½"; 1½" (1.3; 2.5; 1.3; 3.8cm)
Direction:	anticlockwise
Rounds:	4
Finished size:	13" x 13" (33 x 33cm)

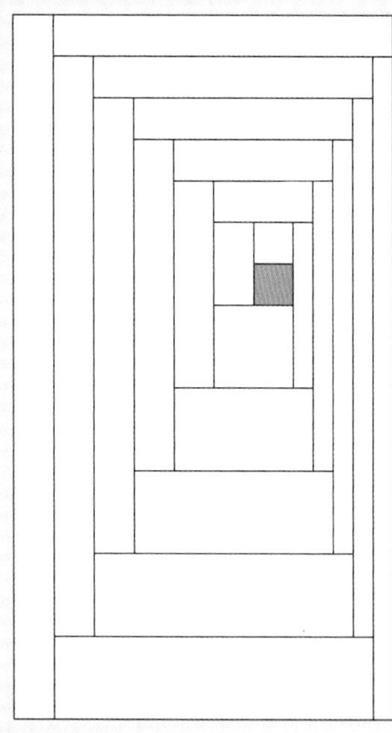

54

Difficulty: 2
Centre: 1" x 1" (2.5 x 2.5cm)
Logs: 1"; 1"; 2"; ½" (2.5; 2.5; 5.1; 1.3cm)
Direction: anticlockwise
Rounds: 6
Finished size: 9½" x 17" (24.1 x 43.2cm)

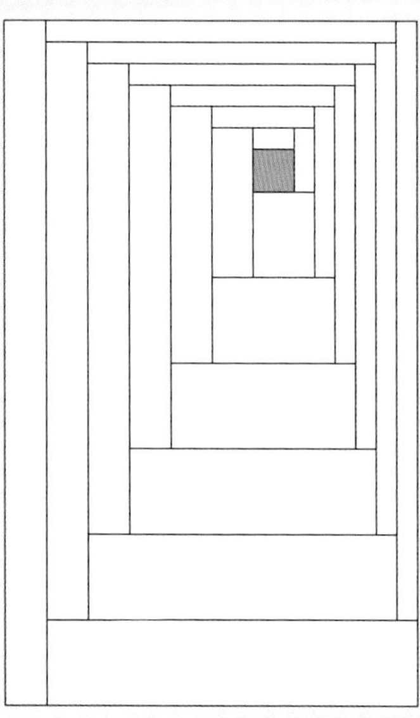

55

Difficulty: 2
Centre: 1" x 1" (2.5 x 2.5cm)
Logs: ½"; ½"; 1"; 2"(1.3; 1.3; 2.5; 5.1cm)
Direction: clockwise
Rounds: 6
Seams: ironed outwards
Finished size: 10" x 16" (25.4 x 40.6cm)

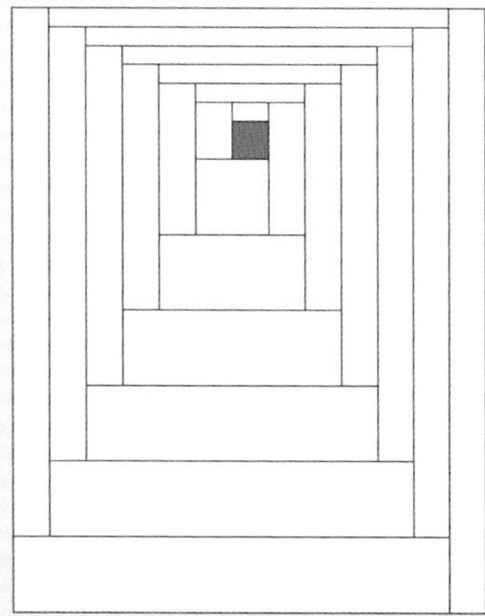

56

Difficulty: 2
Centre: 1" x 1" (2.5 x 2.5cm)
Logs: ½"; 1"; 2"; 1" (1.3; 2.5; 5.1; 2.5cm)
Direction: anticlockwise
Rounds: 6
Finished size: 13" x 16" (33 x 40.6cm)

Multiple Widths (four or more) (pages 142–145)

Width of logs listed from first log to fourth, in the order they were sewn around the centre.

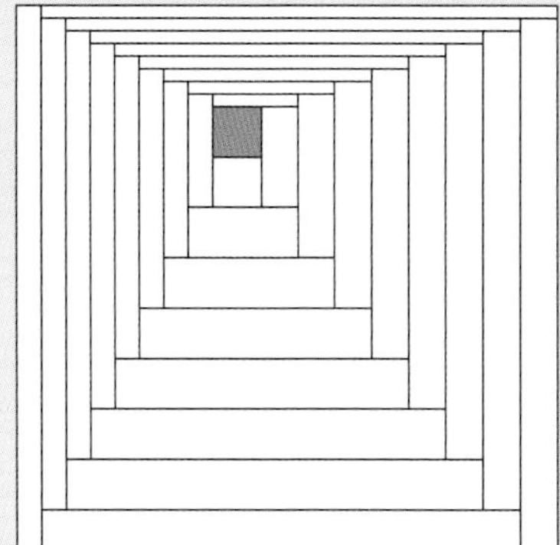

57

Difficulty: 2
Centre: 1" x 1" (2.5 x 2.5cm)
Logs: 1"; ¾"; ¼"; ½" (2.5; 1.9; 0.6; 1.3cm)
Direction: anticlockwise
Rounds: 8
Seams: ironed outwards
Finished size: 11" x 11" (28 x 28cm)

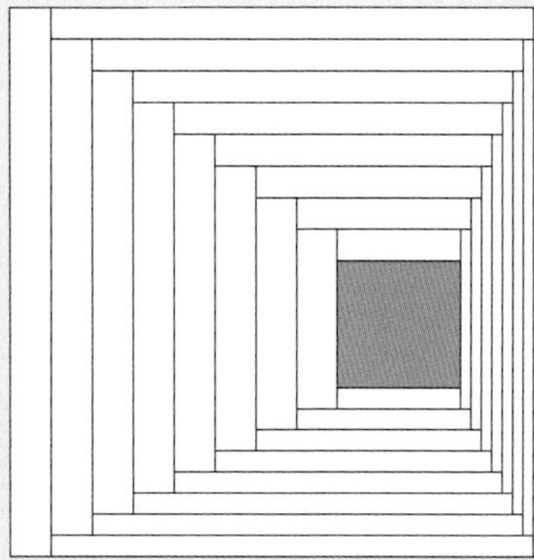

58

Difficulty: 2
Centre: 3" x 3" (7.6 x 7.6cm)
Logs: ½"; ¾" (1.3; 1.9cm) on opposite sides & ¼"; 1" (1.3; 2.5cm) on opposite sides
Direction: *courthouse steps
Rounds: 8
Technique: fabric foundation piecing
Finished size: 13" x 13" (33 x 33cm)

* Inspired by Josef Albers' '*Homage to the Square*' series (1950–1976)

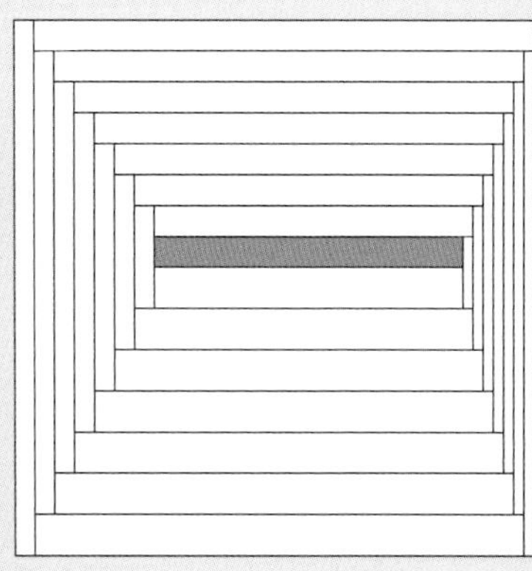

59

Difficulty: 2
Centre: ¾" x 7¾" (1.9 x 19.7cm)
Logs: 1"; ¼"; ¾"; ½" (2.5; 0.6; 1.9; 1.3cm)
Direction: anticlockwise
Rounds: 7
Seams: ¼" & ½" (0.6 & 1.3cm) logs ironed outwards
Finished size: 13" x 13" (33 x 33cm)

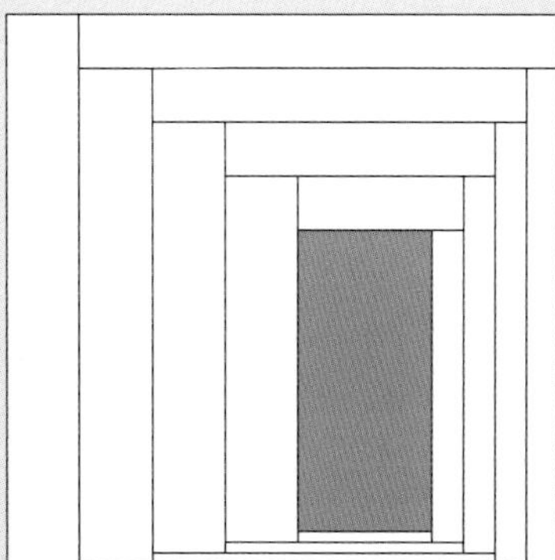

60

Difficulty: 2
Centre: 3" x 7" (7.6 x 17.8cm)
Logs: ¼"; ¾"; 1¼"; 1¾" (0.6; 1.9; 3.2; 4.4cm)
Direction: anticlockwise
Rounds: 4
Finished size: 13" x 13" (33 x 33cm)

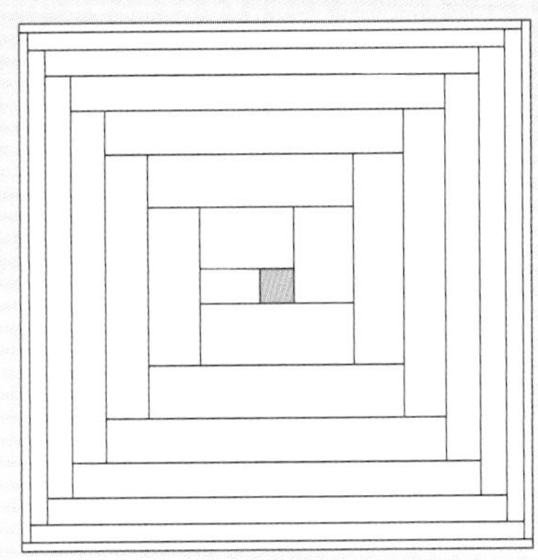

61

Difficulty:	2
Centre:	1" x 1" (2.5 x 2.5cm)
Logs:	width decreases by ¼" (0.6cm) with each round: 1¾"; 1½"; 1¼"; 1"; ¾"; ½"; ¼" (4.4; 3.8; 3.2; 2.5; 1.9; 1.3; 0.6cm)
Direction:	clockwise
Rounds:	7
Finished size:	15" x 15" (38.1 x 38.1cm)

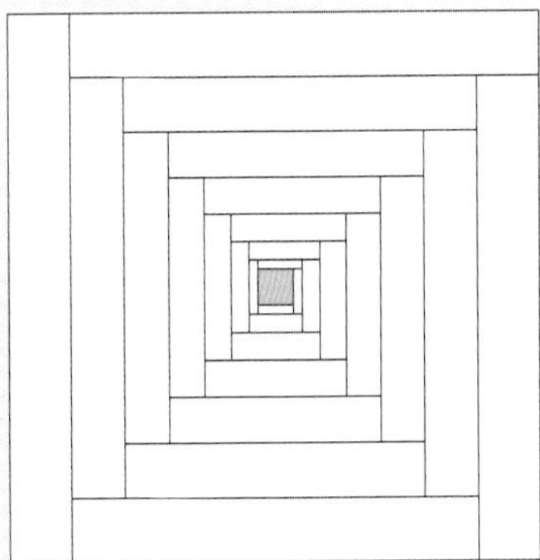

62

Difficulty:	2
Centre:	1" x 1" (2.5 x 2.5cm)
Logs:	width increases by ¼" (0.6cm) with each round: ¼"; ½"; ¾"; 1"; 1¼"; 1½"; 1¾" (0.6; 1.3; 1.9; 2.5; 3.2; 3.8; 4.4cm)
Direction:	clockwise
Rounds:	7
Finished size:	15" x 15" (38.1 x 38.1cm)

Quarter Log Cabin Variations (pages 161–162)

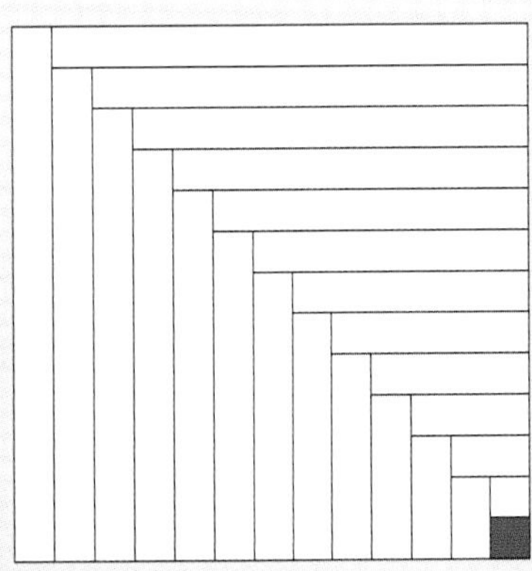

63

Difficulty:	1
Centre:	1" x 1" (2.5 x 2.5cm)
Logs:	1" (2.5cm)
Direction:	anticlockwise
Rounds:	12
Finished size:	13" x 13" (33 x 33cm)

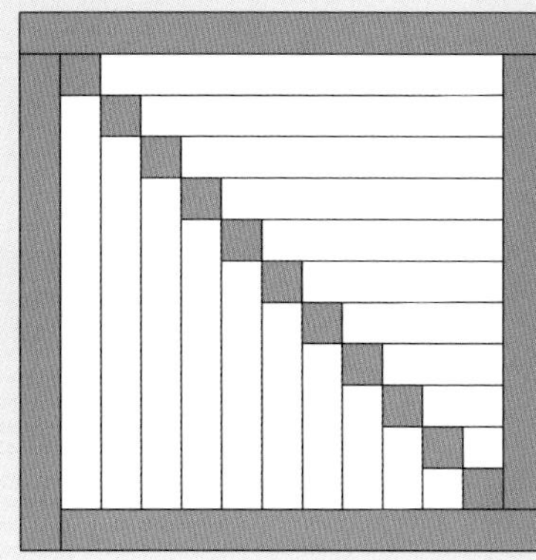

64

—

Difficulty:	3
Centre:	1" x 1" (2.5 x 2.5cm)
Logs:	1" (2.5cm)
Cornerstones:	1" x 1" (2.5 x 2.5cm)
Direction:	clockwise
Rounds:	10
Border:	1" (2.5cm)
Finished size:	13" x 13" (33 x 33cm)

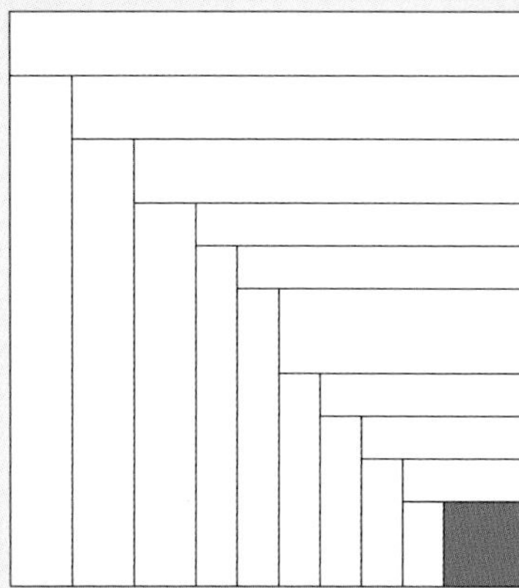

65

—

Difficulty:	2
Centre:	2" x 2" (5.1 x 5.1cm)
Logs:	1" (2.5cm) for 6 rounds then 1½" for 3 rounds + one disrupting log of 2" (5.1cm)
Direction:	clockwise
Rounds:	9
Finished size:	12½" x 13½" (31.8 x 34.3cm)

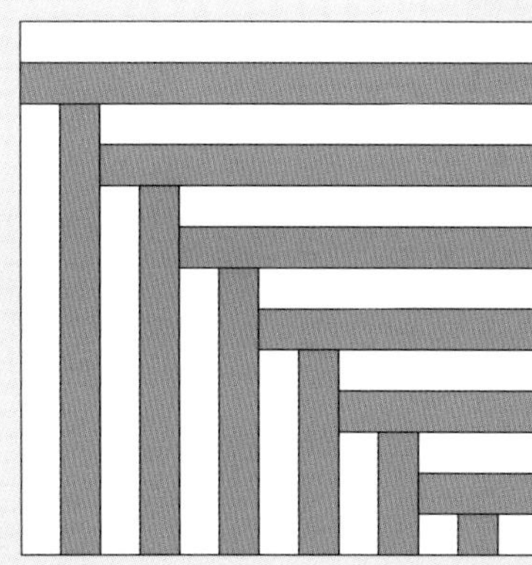

66

—

Difficulty:	2
Centre:	1" x 1" (2.5 x 2.5cm)
Logs:	1" + 1" (2.5 + 2.5cm) double line
Direction:	clockwise
Rounds:	6
Finished size:	13" x 13" (33 x 33cm)

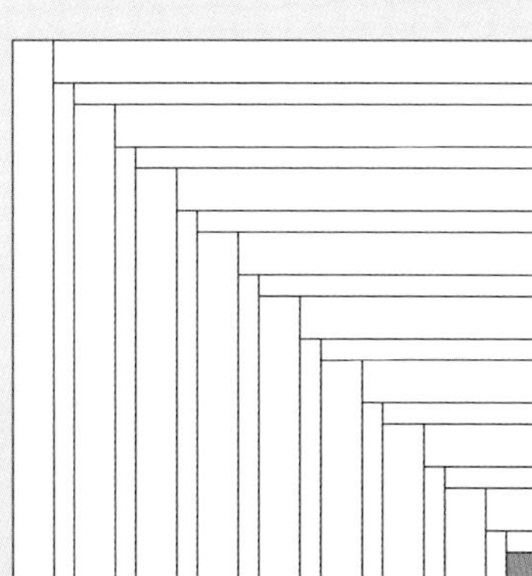

67

—

Difficulty:	2
Centre:	1" x 1" (2.5 x 2.5cm)
Logs:	½" & 1" (1.3 & 2.5cm) alternating (not pre-pieced double line)
Direction:	anticlockwise
Rounds:	16
Finished size:	13" x 13" (33 x 33cm)

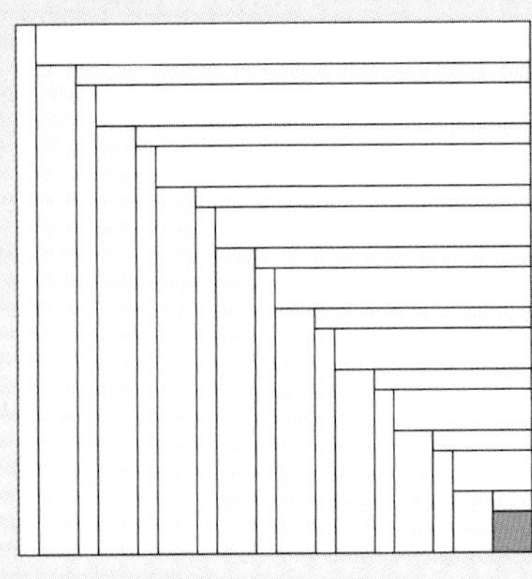

68

Difficulty: 2
Centre: 1" x 1" (2.5 x 2.5cm)
Logs: ½" & 1" (1.3 & 2.5cm) alternating (both within and between rounds)
Direction: anticlockwise
Rounds: 16
Seams: ironed outwards
Finished size: 13" x 13" (33 x 33cm)

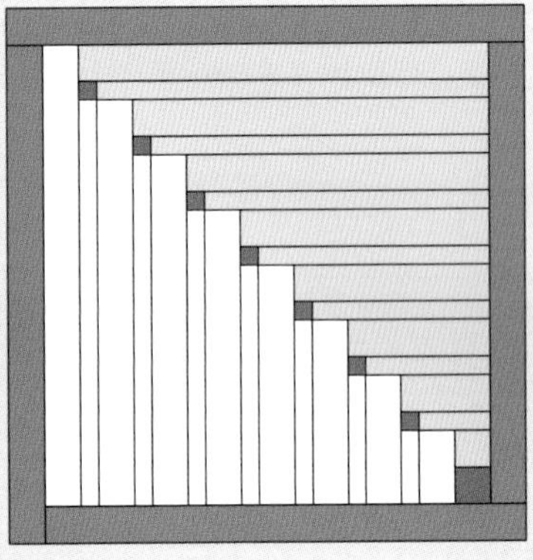

69

Difficulty: 4
Centre: 1" x 1" (2.5 x 2.5cm)
Logs: ½" & 1" (1.3 & 2.5cm) alternating
Direction: anticlockwise
Cornerstones: ½" x ½" (1.3 x 1.3cm) on one side, narrow logs only
Rounds: 15
Border: 1" (2.5cm)
Finished size: 13½" x 13½" (34.3 x 34.3cm)

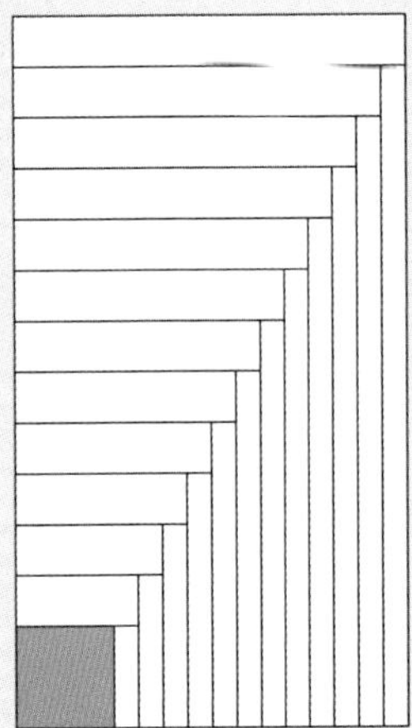

70

Difficulty: 2
Centre: 2" x 2" (5.1 x 5.1cm)
Logs: ½" & 1" (1.3 & 2.5cm)
Direction: anticlockwise
Rounds: 12
Seams: ironed outwards
Finished size: 8" x 14" (20.3 x 35.6cm)

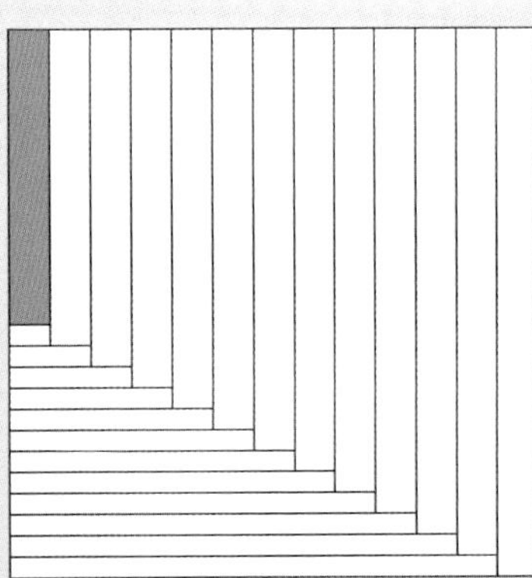

71

Difficulty: 2
Centre: 1" x 7" (2.5 x 17.8cm)
Logs: ½" & 1" (1.3 & 2.5cm)
Direction: anticlockwise
Rounds: 12
Finished size: 13" x 13" (33 x 33cm)

Three-Quarter Log Cabin Variations (pages 161–162)

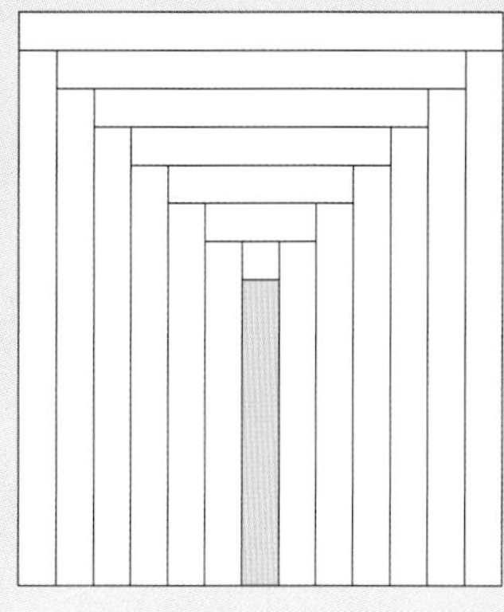

72

Difficulty:	2
Centre:	1" x 7" (2.5 x 17.8cm)
Logs:	1" (2.5cm)
Direction:	top then both sides (first log is 1" x 1" (2.5 x 2.5cm) square)
Rounds:	7 at the top; 6 on the sides
Seams:	ironed outwards
Finished size:	13" x 14" (33 x 35.6cm)

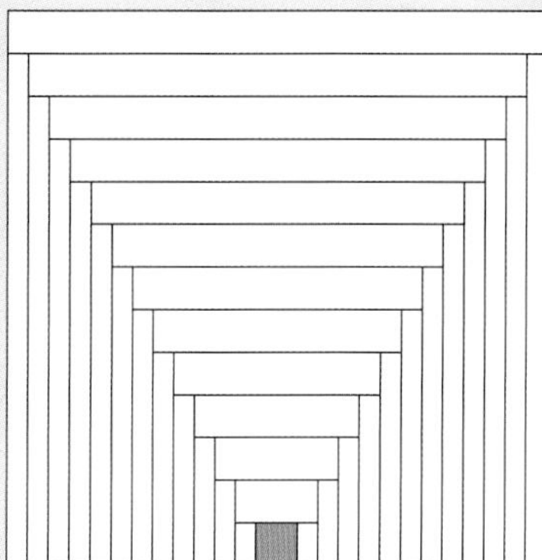

73

Difficulty:	2
Centre:	1" x 1" (2.5 x 2.5cm)
Logs:	½"; ½"; 1" (1.3; 1.3; 2.5cm)
Direction:	both sides then top
Rounds:	12
Technique:	fabric foundation piecing
Finished size:	13" x 13" (33 x 33cm)

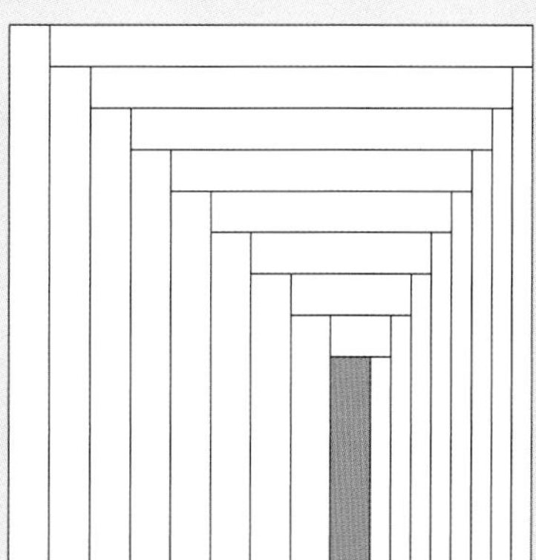

74

Difficulty:	2
Centre:	1" x 5½" (2.5 x 14cm)
Logs:	½"; 1"; 1" (1.3; 2.5; 2.5cm)
Direction:	anticlockwise
Rounds:	8
Finished size:	13" x 13½" (33 x 34.3cm)

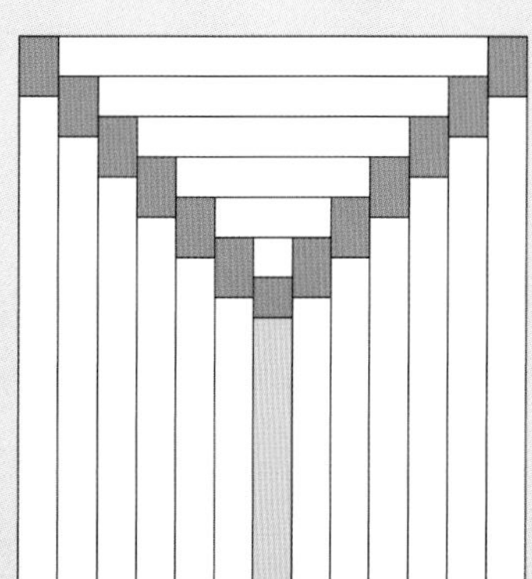

75

Difficulty:	3
Centre:	1" x 7" (2.5 x 17.8cm)
Logs:	1" (2.5cm)
Cornerstones:	on centre and vertical logs (overlapping)
Direction:	top then both sides (first log is 1" x 1" (2.5 x 2.5cm) square)
Rounds:	6
Finished size:	13" x 13½" (33 x 34.3cm)

Polygon and Crazy Log Cabin Variations (pages 165–167)

All polygons are made using the fabric foundation piecing method. The number of logs on each side is likely to vary – especially if the centre is positioned off-centre – and the final dimensions are going to be determined by the size of your foundation fabric. The diagrams below may differ from the original blocks, especially for the crazy log cabins, which are improvised.

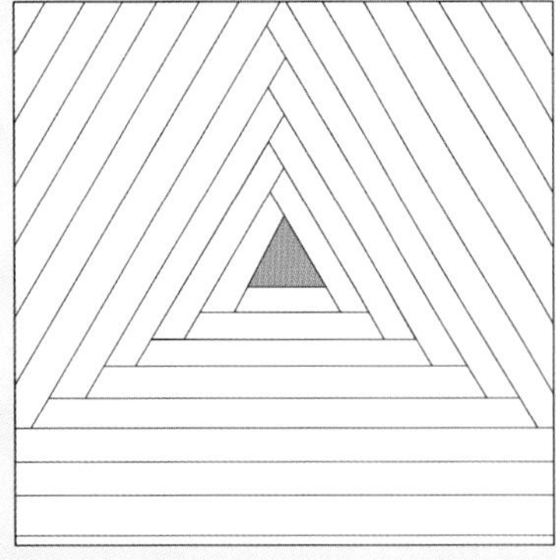

76

Difficulty: 3
Centre: 3" x 3" x 3" (7.6 x 7.6 x 7.6cm) triangle
Logs: ¾" (1.9cm)
Direction: anticlockwise
Rounds: 11
Technique: fabric foundation piecing
Finished size: 13" x 13" (33 x 33cm)

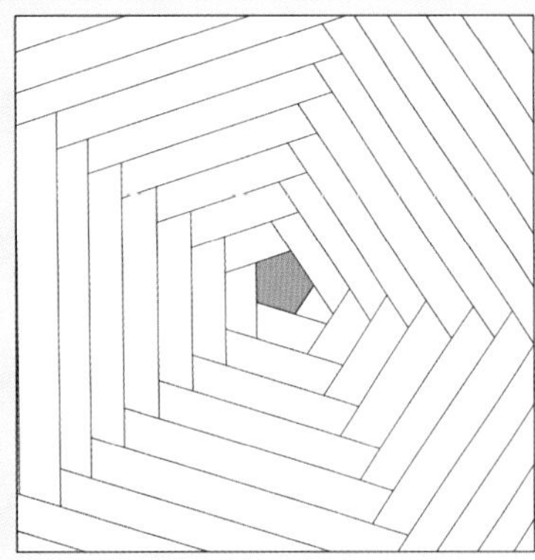

77

Difficulty: 3
Centre: pentagon with 1½" (3.8cm) sides (irregular)
Logs: ¾" (1.9cm)
Direction: clockwise
Rounds: 10
Technique: fabric foundation piecing
Finished size: 13" x 13" (33 x 33cm)

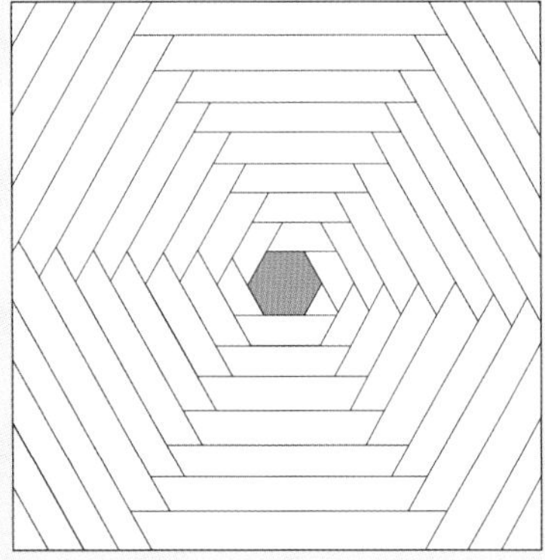

78

Difficulty: 3
Centre: hexagon with ½" (1.3cm) sides
Logs: ¾" (1.9cm)
Direction: clockwise
Rounds: 11
Technique: fabric foundation piecing
Finished size: 13" x 13" (33 x 33cm)

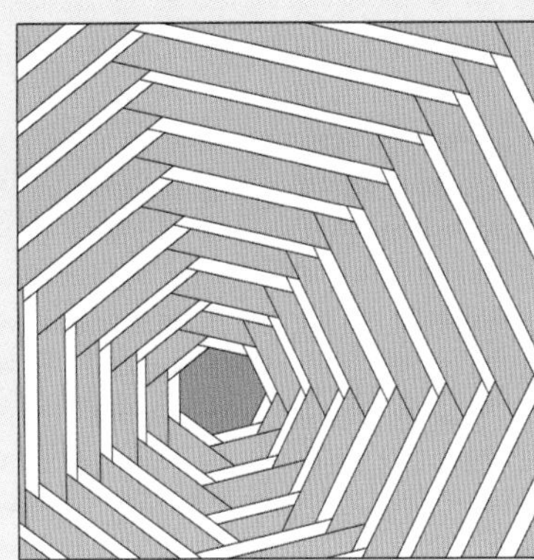

79

Difficulty:	3
Centre:	heptagon with 1" (2.5cm) sides
Logs:	¼" & 1" (0.6 & 2.5cm) alternating
Direction:	clockwise
Rounds:	18
Technique:	fabric foundation piecing
Finished size:	13" x 13" (33 x 33cm)

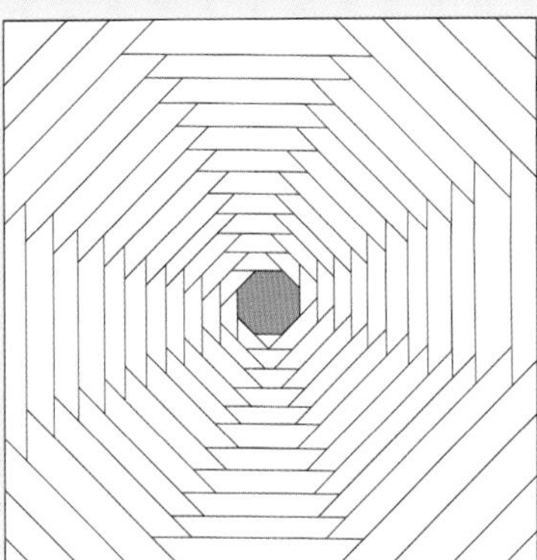

80

Difficulty:	4
Centre:	octagon with ½" (1.3cm) sides
Logs:	½" (1.3cm) for 8 rounds, then 1" (2.5cm) for remaining rounds
Direction:	clockwise
Rounds:	14
Technique:	fabric foundation piecing
Finished size:	13" x 13" (33 x 33cm)

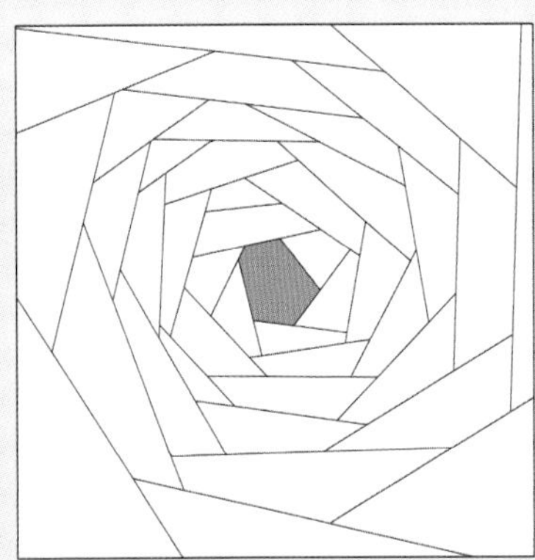

81

Difficulty:	2
Centre:	1½" x ½" (3.8 x 1.3cm) irregular
Logs:	made with fabric scraps ranging from ½" (1.3cm) wide to 2" (5.1cm)
Direction:	clockwise (irregular)
Rounds:	8 (irregular)
Technique:	fabric foundation piecing
Finished size:	13" x 13" (33 x 33cm)

82

Difficulty:	3
Centre:	1½" x ½" (3.8 x 1.3cm) irregular
Logs:	made with fabric scraps ranging from ½" (1.3cm) wide to 2" (5.1cm) + ¼" (0.6cm) double line
Direction:	clockwise (irregular)
Rounds:	6 (irregular)
Technique:	fabric foundation piecing
Finished size:	13" x 13" (33 x 33cm)

Full Circle Log Cabin Variations (and Two Broken Circles) (pages 168–170)

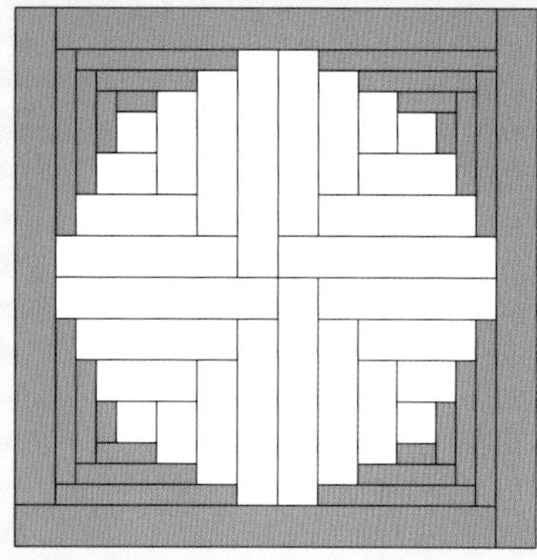

83

Difficulty: 4
Centres: 1" x 1" (2.5 x 2.5cm)
Logs: ½" (1.3cm) for 2 sides & 1" (2.5cm) for 2 sides
Direction: anticlockwise
Rounds: 3
Border: 1" (2.5cm)
Finished size: 13" x 13" (33 x 33cm)

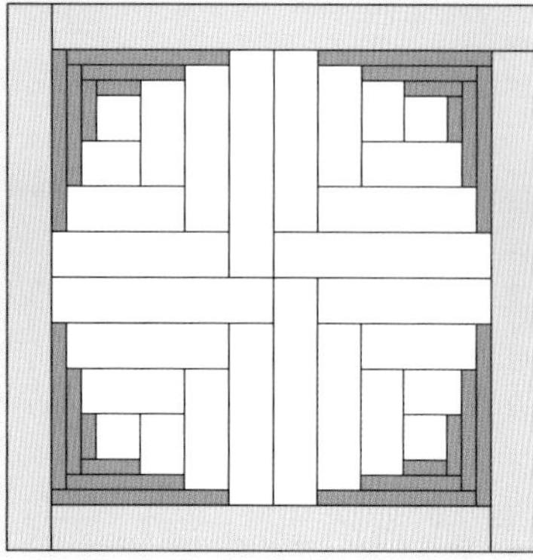

84

Difficulty: 4
Centres: 1" x 1" (2.5 x 2.5cm)
Logs: ⅓" (1cm) for 2 sides & 1" (2.5cm) for 2 sides
Direction: anticlockwise
Rounds: 3
Border: 1" (2.5cm)
Finished size: 12" x 12" (30.5 x 30.5cm)

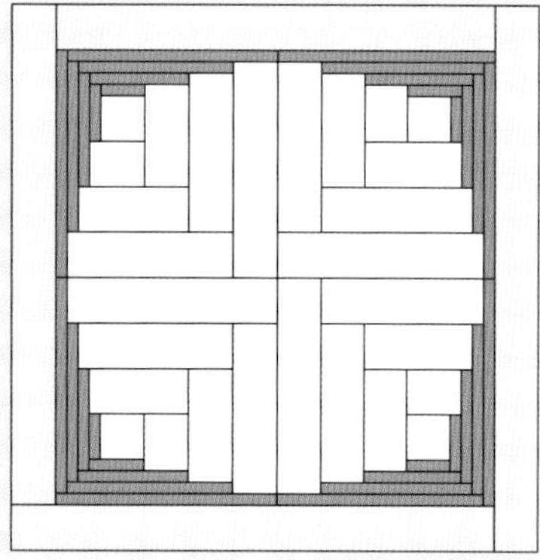

85

Difficulty: 4
Centres: 1" x 1" (2.5 x 2.5cm)
Logs: ¼" (0.6cm) for 2 sides & 1" (2.5cm) for 2 sides
Direction: anticlockwise
Rounds: 4 of narrow logs & 3 of wide logs
Border: 1" (2.5cm)
Seams: narrow logs ironed outwards
Finished size: 12" x 12" (30.5 x 30.5cm)

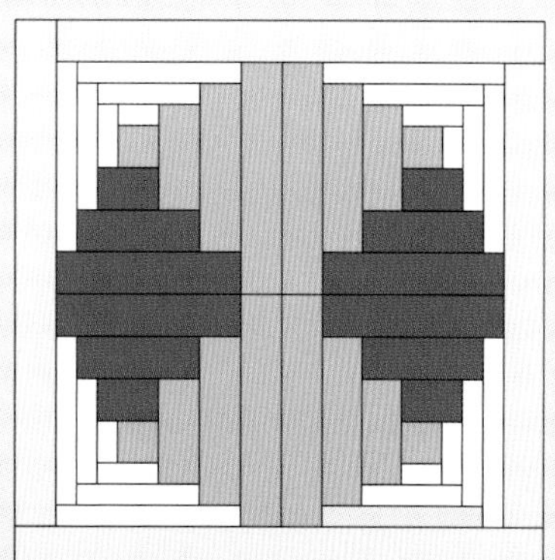

86

Difficulty: 4
Centres: 1" x 1" (2.5 x 2.5cm)
Logs: ½" (1.3cm) for 2 sides & 1" (2.5cm) for 2 sides
Direction: *anticlockwise for two blocks & *clockwise for 2 blocks (logs sewn in the same order of colours)
Rounds: 3
Border: 1" (2.5cm)
Finished size: 13" x 13" (33 x 33cm)

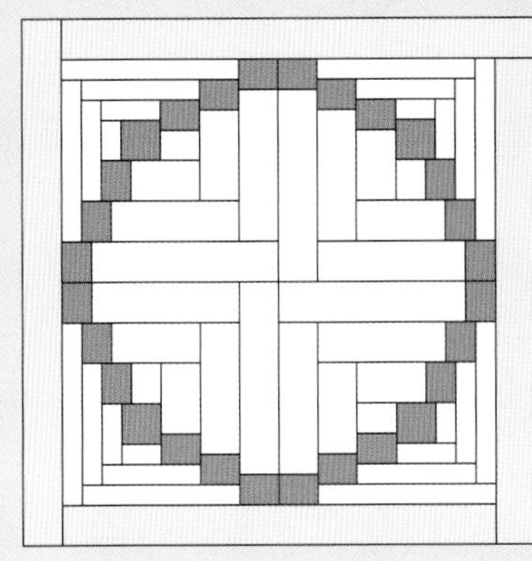

87

Difficulty: 4
Centres: 1" x 1" (2.5 x 2.5cm) (same colour as cornerstones)
Logs: ½" (1.3cm) for 2 sides & 1" (2.5cm) for 2 sides
Cornerstones: on wide logs (overlapping)
Direction: clockwise
Rounds: 3
Border: 1" (2.5cm)
Finished size: 13" x 13" (33 x 33cm)

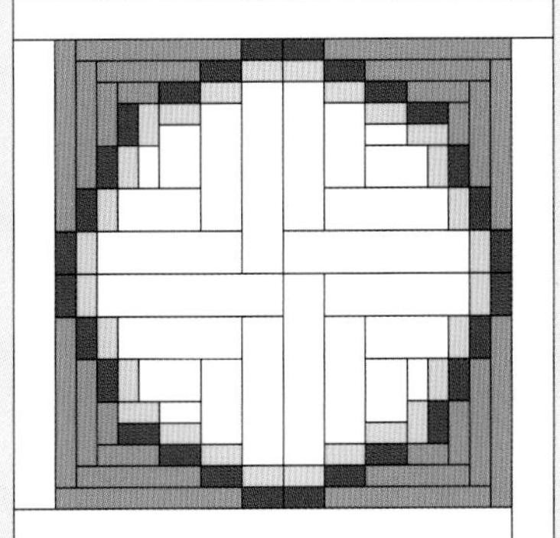

88

Difficulty: 4
Centres: 1" x 1" (2.5 x 2.5cm) (pieced, same as cornerstones)
Logs: ½" (1.3cm) for 2 sides & 1" (2.5cm) for 2 sides
Cornerstones: 1" x 1" (2.5 x 2.5cm) on wide logs, from pre-pieced ½" + ½" (1.3 + 1.3cm) double line strip
Direction: anticlockwise
Rounds: 3
Border: 1" (2.5cm)
Finished size: 13" x 13" (33 x 33cm)

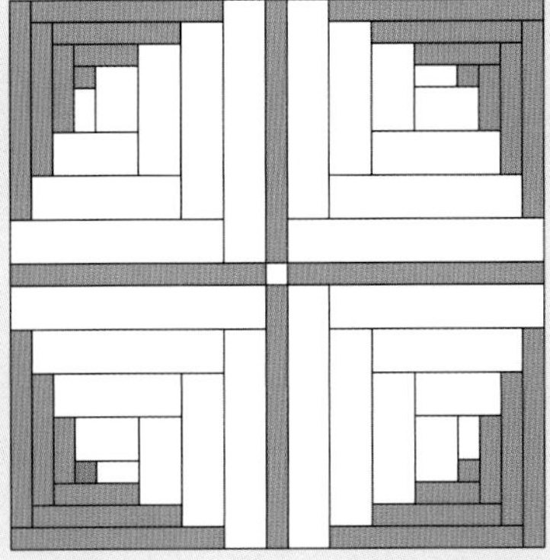

89

Difficulty: 4
Centres: ½" x ½" (1.3 x 1.3cm)
Logs: 1" (2.5cm) for 2 sides & ½" (1.3cm) for 2 sides
Direction: anticlockwise
Rounds: 4 of wide logs & 3 of narrow logs
Sashing: ½" (1.3cm) with contrasting ½" x ½" (1.3 x 1.3cm) centre cornerstone
Finished size: 12½" x 12½" (31.8 x 31.8cm)

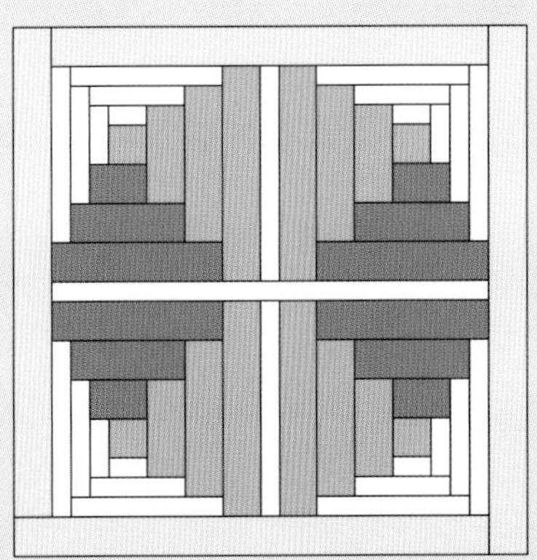

90

Difficulty: 4
Centres: 1" x 1" (2.5 x 2.5cm)
Logs: ½" (1.3cm) for 2 sides & 1" (2.5cm) for 2 sides
Direction: *anticlockwise for 2 blocks & *clockwise for 2 blocks (logs sewn in the same order of colours)
Rounds: 3
Sashing: ½" (1.3cm)
Border: 1" (2.5cm)
Finished size: 13½" x 13½" (34.3 x 34.3cm)

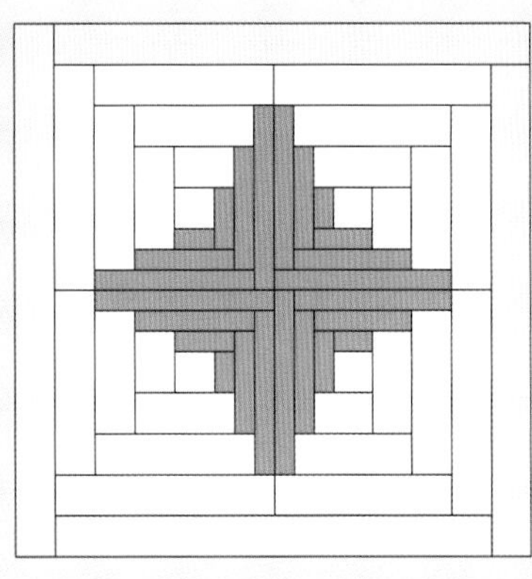

91

Difficulty:	4
Centres:	1" x 1" (2.5 x 2.5cm)
Logs:	½" (1.3cm) for 2 sides & 1" (2.5cm) for 2 sides
Direction:	anticlockwise
Rounds:	3
Border:	1" (2.5cm)
Seams:	narrow logs ironed inwards
Finished size:	13" x 13" (33 x 33cm)

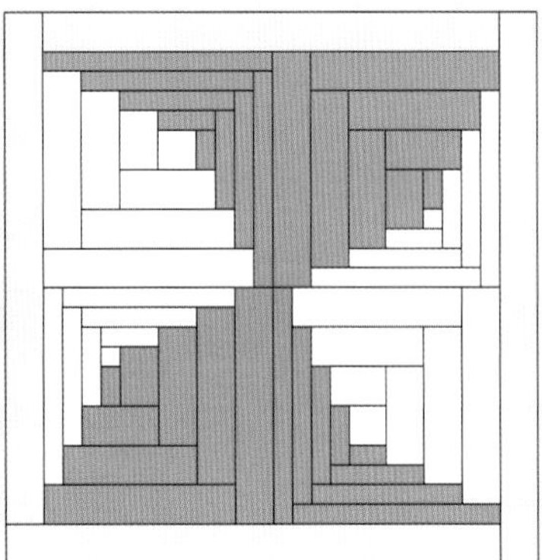

92

Difficulty: 4+

2 blocks (top left & bottom right):

Centres:	1" x 1" (2.5 x 2.5cm)
Logs:	½" (1.3cm) for 2 sides & 1" (2.5cm) for 2 sides
Rounds:	4 of narrow logs & 3 of wide logs

2 blocks (top right & bottom left):

Centre:	½" x ½" (1.3 x 1.3cm)
Logs:	1" (2.5cm) for 2 sides & ½" (1.3cm) for 2 sides
Rounds:	4 of wide logs & 3 of narrow logs

Direction:	anticlockwise (all blocks)
Border:	1" (2.5cm)
Seams:	ironed outwards on one half of each block
Finished size:	14" x 14" (35.6 x 35.6cm)

Four Blocks Variations (pages 168–170)

93

Difficulty:	4
Centres:	½" (1.3cm)
Logs:	½" (1.3cm)
Direction:	*courthouse steps
Rounds:	5
Borders:	½" (1.3cm) & 1" (2.5cm)
Seams:	ironed outwards
Finished size:	14" x 14" (35.6 x 35.6cm)

94

—

Difficulty: 4
Centres: ½" x 1" (1.3 x 2.5cm)
Logs: ½" (1.3cm)
Direction: *courthouse steps: start with the striped sections' logs; follow with solid sections' logs
Rounds: 6 for striped sections; 5 for solid sections
Sashing: ½" (1.3cm) between pairs of blocks only (to link stripy sections)
Seams: ironed outwards
Finished size: 12" x 13½" (30.5 x 34.3cm)

* Inspired by a Civil War quilt, Illinois, 1860

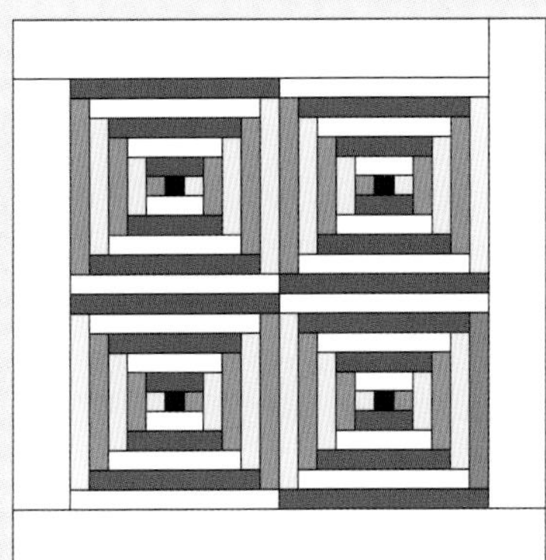

95

—

Difficulty: 4
Centres: ½" x ½" (1.3 x 1.3cm)
Logs: ½" (1.3cm)
Direction: *courthouse steps
Rounds: 5
Border: 1½" (3.8cm)
Seams: ironed outwards
Finished size: 14" x 14" (35.6 x 35.6cm)

* Inspired by an 'Interwoven Log Cabin', source unknown

96

—

Difficulty: 4
Centres: 1" x 1" (2.5 x 2.5cm)
Logs: ½" (1.3cm)
Direction: anticlockwise
Rounds: full first round, then only 2 logs on second round (to offset the centre), then 3 full rounds
Sashing: ½" (1.3cm)
Border: ½" (1.3cm) border
Seams: ironed outwards
Finished size: 12½" x 12½" (31.8 x 31.8cm)

* Inspired by a Mennonite log cabin quilt (1865–1885) from the International Quilt Museum collection

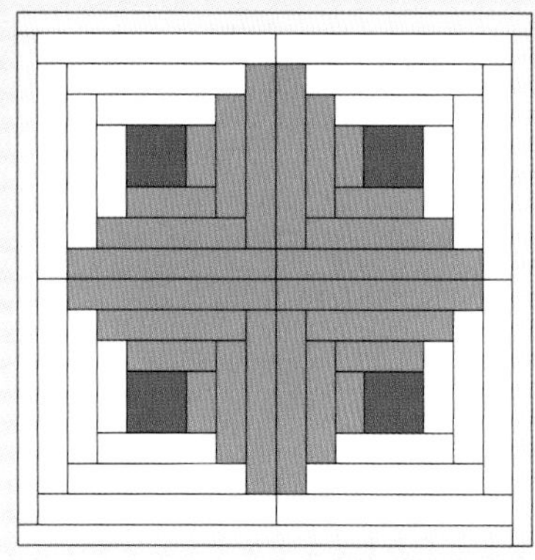

97

Difficulty: 4
Centres: 1½" x 1½" (3.8 x 3.8cm)
Logs: ¾" (1.9cm)
Direction: anticlockwise or clockwise
Rounds: 3
Border: ¾" (1.9cm)
Seams: ironed outwards on two sides
Finished size: 13½" x 13½" (34.3 x 34.3cm)

* Inspired by a log cabin quilt (ca. 1900) from the Metropolitan Museum collection

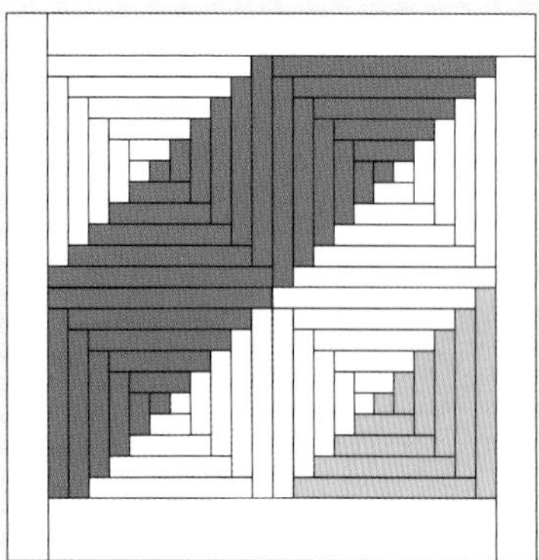

98

Difficulty: 4
Centres: ½" x ½" (1.3 x 1.3cm)
Logs: ½" (1.3cm)
Direction: anticlockwise
Rounds: 5
Border: 1" (2.5cm)
Seams: finger pressed
Finished size: 13" x 13" (33 x 33cm)

* Traditional 'Fields and Furrows' pattern

99

Difficulty: 4
Centres: 2" x 2" (5.1 x 5.1cm)
Logs: ¾" (1.9cm)
Direction: anticlockwise or clockwise
Rounds: 4 (two sides only)
Sashing: 1¼" (3.2cm)
Border: ¾" (1.9cm) (ironed outwards)
Finished size: 13" x 13" (33 x 33cm)

* Inspired by a rug made by Sonia Delaunay (ca. 1912)

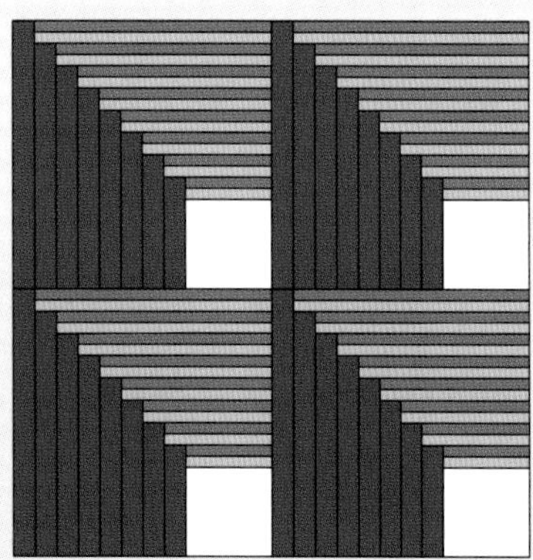

100

Difficulty: 4
Centres: 2" x 2" (5.1 x 5.1cm)
Logs: ½" (1.3cm) & ¼" + ¼" (0.6 + 0.6cm) double line
Direction: *anticlockwise
Rounds: 8 (2 sides only)
Seams: ironed outwards
Finished size: 13" x 13" (33 x 33cm)

SEWING AND QUILTING RESOURCES

Here are a few of my favourite sewing and quilting books, where you can find techniques and ideas for transforming your blocks into quilts, cushions, bags, etc.

Modern Quilting by Julius Arthur of House of Quinn (Hardie Grant, 2021)

Quilt Me! by Jane Brocket (Harper Collins Publishers, 2014)

Free-Form Quilts and Patchwork by Jessie Cutts (Batsford Books, 2026)

The Handmade Home by Arounna Khounnoraj (Quadrille Publishing Limited, 2025)

Farm and Folk Quilt Alchemy by Sara Larson Buscaglia (Abrams, 2023)

Quilts by Denyse Schmidt (Chronicle Books, 2005)

Quilting by Andrea Tsang Jackson (Nine Ten Publications, 2025)

The Improv Handbook for Modern Quilters by Sherri Lynn Wood (STC Craft/A Melanie Falick Book, 2015)

Inspiration

Here's a list of inspiring books on quilts, most of them featuring log cabin quilts. Also look up: Gee's Bend's quilts on the Souls Grown Deep website; American quilter Luke Haynes' log cabin series; and Japanese log cabin quilts.

Gee's Bend: The Architecture of the Quilt edited by Paul Arnett, Joanne Cubbs and Eugene W. Metcalf Jr (Tinwood Books, 2006)

Unconventional & Unexpected: American Quilts Below the Radar, 1950–2000 by Roderick Kiracofe (Schiffer, 2022)

Patchwork: A World Tour by Catherine Legrand (Thames and Hudson, 2022)

Of Salt and Spirit: Black Quilters in the American South by Sharbreon Plummer (University Press of Mississippi, 2024)

Amish Quilts: Crafting an American Icon by Janneken Smucker (John Hopkins University Press, 2017)

Routed West: Twentieth-Century African American Quilts in California edited by Elaine Yau (DelMonico Books, 2025)

ACKNOWLEDGEMENTS

THANK YOU

To Polly Powell, for taking a risk in backing what was, let's be honest, a slightly mad endeavour, and letting me make a book so personal and different. It was huge fun, and I'll be forever grateful for the opportunity.

To the team at Batsford, for their support throughout this project, in particular Bella MacConnol, Nicola Newman, Pete Rouse and Frida Green, as well as Eoghan O'Brien, for bringing this book to life on the page.

To Tom Leighton, for the beautiful photography.

To the students who came to my log cabin workshops, from whom I learned so much, and to Rachel Hart and the team at Ray Stitch. A special shoutout to Jackie Davies for having invented the slashed log cabin.

To Rachel Yuen, Pat Kilduff and Camille Asseraf, for testing the patterns in earlier versions of this book and making invaluable comments and suggestions.

To Adam Herbert, my quilting friend, for his enthusiastic support ever since we met in 2020.

To Instagram friends and followers: your likes, comments and messages through the years mean the world. All the patchwork advice has been most appreciated too.

To friends, family and studio neighbours, for your encouragement and patience each time I took out my phone to show you what I was up to.

To my parents, Liane and Ronald, for raising me in a house where we made things, and my children Rose and Oscar, for cheering me on.

And finally to George, my husband, for buying me that sewing machine nearly 20 years ago, encouraging me to take the plunge and never doubting me. Also, for counting every log of every block to make sure the Block Directory was accurate. If that's not love then I don't know what is.

ABOUT THE AUTHOR

Catherine-Marie Longtin is a Montreal-born French Canadian quilt-maker and textile artist now based in London. She grew up in a family where people made things, and learned to sew from her mother at a young age. As a teenager, she started experimenting with fabrics by sewing bed linens and kitchen textiles. After a PhD in cognitive science and a career in academia that took her from Montreal to Paris, Lyon and Cambridge, she went back to her love of textiles and colours.

Since 2016 she has had a studio in Camberwell, South East London. She does commission work for private clients and sells quilts and artworks online, via open studio events and textile fairs. She teaches various patchwork classes, including a log cabin workshop at Ray Stitch, a fabric shop and haberdashery in North London.

Among Catherine-Marie's earliest influences were her mother's piles of French *Elle Décor*, which fostered a love of beautiful home textiles. Later on, she discovered artists such as Josef and Anni Albers, Mark Rothko, Agnes Martin, Nicolas de Staël and Paul Klee, who became central influences on her work. She's also inspired by quilters who have pushed traditional boundaries to create personal visions of what a quilt can be.

Although many of her pieces are full-size quilts, she enjoys working on a smaller scale and making artworks. She reckons she probably has ideas for another few log cabin blocks.

Photo by Lucinda Newton-Dunn